PILOT TRAINING MANUAL FOR THE

PUBLISHED FOR HEADQUARTERS, AAF

OFFICE OF ASSISTANT CHIEF OF AIR STAFF, TRAINING

BY HEADQUARTERS, AAF, OFFICE OF FLYING SAFETY

Foreword...

This manual is the text for your training as a P-40 pilot.

The Air Forces' most experienced training and supervisory personnel have collaborated to make it a complete exposition of what your pilot duties are, how each duty will be performed, and why it must be performed in the manner prescribed.

The techniques and procedures described in this book are standard and mandatory. In this respect the manual serves the dual purpose of a training checklist and a working handbook. Use it to make sure that you learn everything described herein. Use it to study and review the essential facts concerning everything taught. Such additional self-study and review will not only advance your training, but will alleviate the burden of your already overburdened instructors.

This training manual does not replace the Technical Orders for the airplane, which will always be your primary source of information concerning the P-40 so long as you fly it. This is essentially the textbook of the P-40. Used properly, it will enable you to utilize the pertinent Technical Orders to even greater advantage.

General, U. S. Army
Commanding General
Army Air Forces

INTRODUCTION

You're a fighter pilot now. Your fingers are itching to get at the controls of a P-51 or a P-47. You may be a little disappointed that you have to spend a few weeks flying a P-40.

Well, don't be. When you learn to fly the P-40 there won't be a fighter you can't handle. The P-40 is no cinch to fly; it's fast and skittish and responds like lightning to controls. The savvy you pick up in the P-40 is going to make you a good pilot in any fighter.

And don't think of the P-40 as a sort of glorified advanced trainer. It's a combat airplane. It's still being flown in China, the Pacific and the Mediterranean—and it's still shooting down Japs and Jerries.

True, no more P-40's are being sent to the war theaters. Instead we are sending P-47's, P-51's, P-38's and even newer aircraft. We're sending them for a good reason: they're better aircraft than the P-40. In the air war we must have constant progress if we are to keep winning. The enemy's aircraft have been improved; ours must be even better. So the P-40 has made way for the new fighters.

The P-40 now is like an old champion thoroughbred that's been retired from racing. But what a record of wins the old horse piled up! It's an airplane you can be proud to fly. You know about the Flying Tigers and how they kept the Burma Road open with a handful of P-40's. They were outnumbered, they were fighting against Jap planes that could climb and maneuver better. But the Flying Tigers had superior skill, guts, teamwork, armor and firepower. In their P-40's over Burma they wrote a glorious page in the history of aerial combat.

In other theaters the P-40's score-sheet is also impressive. By actual count, in 50 representative air battles the score of P-40 squadrons against the enemy was 13½ to 1!

The P-40 has been one of the most versatile of aircraft. It has doubled as a light bomber, dive bomber and attack bomber. In 1943, pilots in Burma called them "B-40's" and blasted Jap bridges with 1000-lb. bombs shackled to the belly. Whatever the P-40 has been called upon to do, it has done.

Since the first P-40 in 1940, there have been 14 major modifications and many other less sweeping changes in the airplane. The newest P-40, the N model, represents three years of lessons learned in the hard school of combat.

In 1940 the first P-40's were sent to the British. They called it the Tomahawk. By the end of 1940 the B, C and D series were in England. The D was so different from the earlier models that the British gave it a new name—the Kittyhawk.

In 1941 came the E model. In 1942 the Allison engine was replaced by a Packard-built Rolls-Royce engine in the P-40 F. (This one was called the Warhawk by the British.)

Through 1942 and 1943 modifications continued. The Rolls-Royce was replaced by an improved Allison. Better propeller, hydraulic, electric, fuel, oil and coolant systems were installed. The streamlining was improved. The plane was armored better. Each modification made it a better airplane.

The last few models are about as much like the first P-40 as the 1942 Ford V-8 is like the first Ford V-8. Two years ago the latest P-40's would have been the best fighters in the air. Today they've been passed up by newer fighters.

But they're still the best, fastest, most nervous airplanes **you've** ever flown. It requires all of your skill, all of your concentration, all of your alertness, to master the P-40.

It is worth the sweat and study. Remember—if you're a good P-40 pilot, you're a good fighter pilot.

THIS IS THE P-40

Span . . . . . 37 ft. 4 in.
Length . . . . . 33 ft. 4 in.
Height . . . . . 12 ft. 7 in.

The P-40 airplane, built by Curtiss-Wright, is a single-place, all-metal, low-wing monoplane, powered with one Allison engine which drives a 3-bladed Curtiss Electric constant-speed propeller.

The flaps, brakes and conventional landing gear operate hydraulically. Rudder, ailerons and elevators are constructed of fabric-covered metal and have metal trim tabs. The cockpit is covered with a sliding plexiglas canopy and protected in front by a bulletproof windshield.

The P-40 is armed with six free-firing .50 cal. machine guns, three in each wing. Each wing also has shackles for carrying one bomb or an auxiliary gas tank. The belly shackle can carry a 500 or 1000 lb. bomb or a fuel tank ranging from 52 to 150 gallons in capacity.

Operation and Description

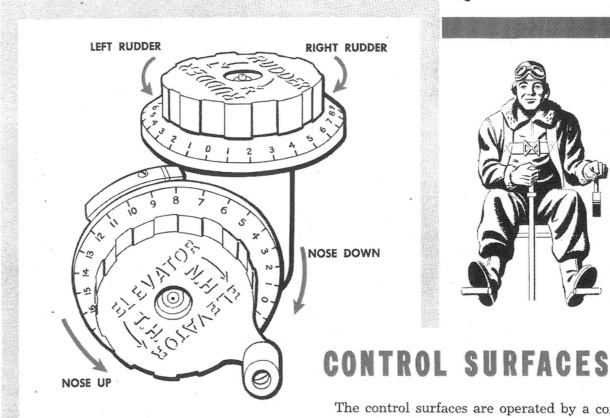

LEFT RUDDER

RIGHT RUDDER

NOSE DOWN

NOSE UP

CONTROL SURFACES

The control surfaces are operated by a conventional pistol-grip stick and adjustable rudder pedals. Elevators and rudder trim tab controls are on the left side of the cockpit forward of the flap control lever. The rudder trim tab control is a round knob, marked in degrees beginning with zero in the neutral position, which turns in either direction. The elevator trim tab is also a round knob, similarly calibrated. It is located in a vertical position below the rudder trim tab control and is controlled by a small hand crank. The flap controls are on the left side of the cockpit above the landing gear handle.

The aileron trim tab must be adjusted manually on the ground, except on some models which have an electric aileron trim tab control.

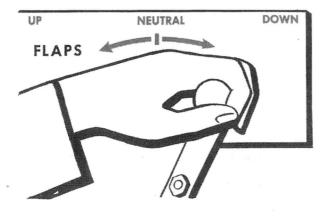

UP   NEUTRAL   DOWN

FLAPS

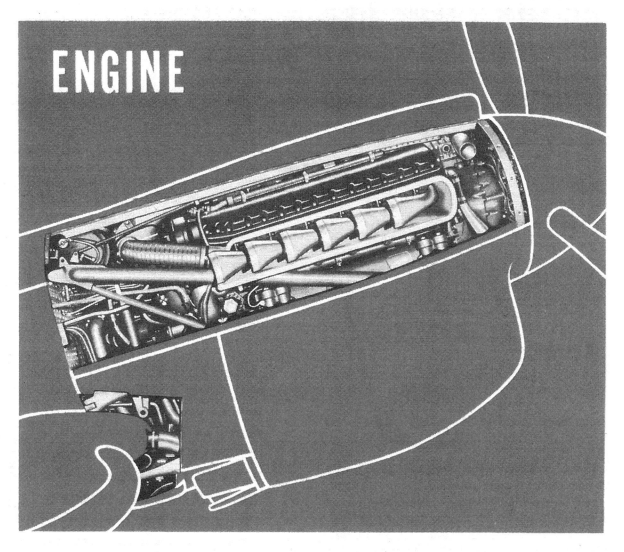

ENGINE

The 1150-Hp Allison V-1710, a 12-cylinder, V-type, liquid-cooled engine, has a single-speed internal blower and integral reduction gears through which the propeller is driven. Models starting with the P-40 K have a manifold pressure regulator which automatically maintains constant manifold pressure up to 12,000 feet and eliminates the need for resetting the throttle with altitude changes. Above 12,000 feet the effectiveness of the regulator drops sharply.

The Allison is a good, tough engine, but like all precision instruments it requires proper treatment. You, as pilot, are the controlling factor in how long the engine lasts, how well it operates. If you mistreat the engine, you can be sure of paying for your carelessness.

Watch your prop and throttle settings. Excessive manifold pressure and rpm cause the engine to detonate.

Detonation is an explosion in the cylinder head. The normal burning wave, as it travels across the cylinder head, subjects the unburned portion of the fuel charge to tremendous temperatures and pressures. If these forces are great enough, the remaining fuel charge explodes before it can burn, and the shock waves from this explosion rob your engine of power. If the waves are strong enough, they can blow the cylinder heads off the engine.

As long as you remain within the normal operating limits of the engine, you run no risk of detonation.

High oil and coolant temperatures can also cause detonation. These, then, are two more things you must guard against.

Always make power changes smoothly and evenly. This engine won't absorb a sudden blast of power without acting up.

Move the controls slowly and smoothly to the desired settings instead of trying to pick up the proper setting with one swift movement.

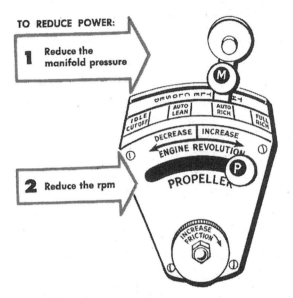

If you reduce the rpm first, you get a jump in manifold pressure which can cause detonation if the relation of rpm to manifold pressure is greatly altered. An engine running at constant power settings receives a constant amount of fuel and air from the blower. If you lower the rpm and the manifold pressure remains constant, the blower continues to supply the same fuel-air charge. The engine, running at a slower speed, cannot absorb this charge. As a result, pressures in the blower and cylinder heads build up and cause detonation. Therefore, never reduce rpm before manifold pressure.

TO INCREASE POWER:

1 Increase the rpm

2 Advance the throttle.

If you advance the throttle before you increase the rpm, the same thing happens as when you reduce rpm before manifold pressure in decreasing power.

As the engine picks up speed, the manifold pressure drops. This is a normal and desired reaction. **Note:** Above 12,000 feet, increased rpm gives you **increased** manifold pressure.

The P-40 F and L models are powered with Packard Rolls-Royce engines. For standardization purposes many of these have been replaced with Allisons. P-40 F and L models which have been refitted with Allisons are called P-40 R-1's and P-40 R-2's respectively.

ALL POWER SETTINGS GIVEN IN THIS MANUAL ARE FOR ALLISON ENGINES AND GRADE 100 FUEL. IN MANY CASES THE SETTING FOR OPERATING WITH GRADE 91 FUEL IS THE SAME AS THAT FOR GRADE 100. WHEN THERE IS A DIFFERENCE, THE SETTING FOR GRADE 91 IS STATED IN PARENTHESES AFTER THE SETTING FOR GRADE 100.

POWER SETTINGS FOR THE ROLLS-ROYCE ENGINE ARE GIVEN IN TABLES ON PAGES 46 AND 48.

ROLLS-ROYCE ENGINE SUPERCHARGER

The Rolls-Royce engine which powers the P-40 F and L models has a single stage 2-speed supercharger controlled by a lever on the bottom of the throttle quadrant. The lever has two positions—HIGH and LOW. To get the best power, operate the engine with the supercharger in LOW below 1200 feet and in HIGH above 1200 feet.

To move the blower from LOW to HIGH or from HIGH to LOW, reduce the manifold pressure to 20″ Hg. and the rpm to 2000, and then quickly shift the lever into the desired position. You can shift the supercharger lever without first reducing power, but this practice is not recommended except in emergencies because it is hard on the supercharger clutch. In normal operation, first reduce power.

Except for the supercharger, there are no great differences in the power and operation of Rolls-Royce and Allison engines.

ENGINE CONTROLS and INSTRUMENTS

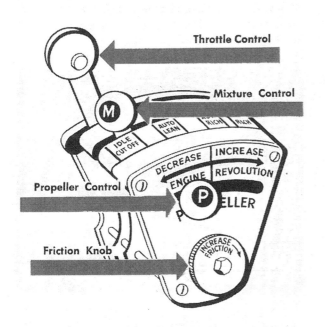

THROTTLE QUADRANT

The throttle quadrant consists of throttle, mixture, and propeller controls. Adjusting the friction knob on the side of the throttle quadrant prevents the three control levers from creeping.

A. The mixture control has four positions: IDLE CUT-OFF, AUTO LEAN, AUTO RICH, and FULL RICH. When the mixture control lever is in AUTO RICH or AUTO LEAN, altitude mixture control is automatically maintained. Always start the engine in IDLE CUT-OFF to prevent flooding and to reduce fire hazard.

Note: Never use the FULL RICH position except:

1. When the AUTO LEAN or AUTO RICH rubber diaphragm breaks or the automatic compensating aneroid fails. Symptoms are spitting or cutting out of the engine. In high-speed dives from high altitudes, there may be diaphragm or aneroid trouble.

2. When engine detonates. Before you move the mixture control level to FULL RICH, reduce power as much as possible.

B. The propeller control lever is pushed forward to increase rpm, pulled backward to decrease rpm.

Note: On P-40 N models with prop and throttle linkage the propeller lever cannot be moved. Throttle action automatically increases and decreases rpm.

IGNITION SWITCH

This is a conventional switch with the usual four positions: OFF, L, R, and BOTH.

STARTER

P-40's have one of three types of starters:

A. The usual foot-operated pedal with EN-ERGIZE, ENGAGE, and OFF positions.

B. A toggle switch below the throttle quadrant with the same three positions.

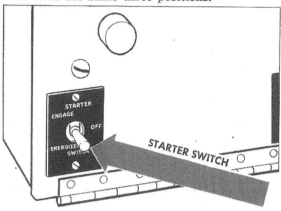

C. P-40 F and L models have direct-drive starters.

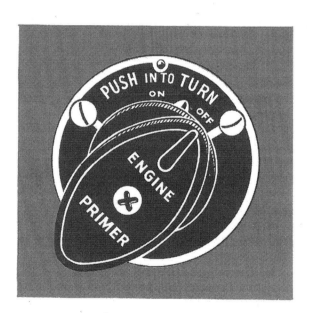

ENGINE PRIMER

The primer is below the dashboard. Unlock the pump by turning the handle counter-clock-

wise to ON. Lock by pushing the handle in and turning clock-wise to OFF.

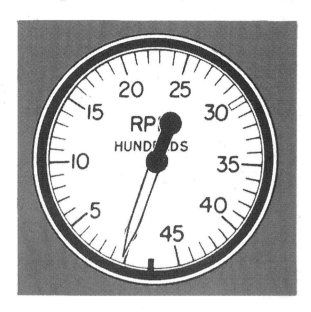

TACHOMETER

The speed of the engine is indicated in revolutions per minute on a tachometer calibrated in hundreds of rpm up to 45.

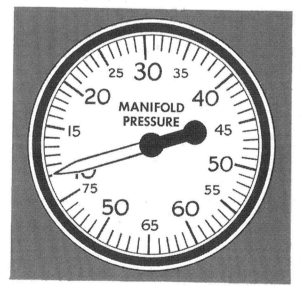

MANIFOLD PRESSURE GAGE

This gage is calibrated in inches of mercury ranging from 10" to 75".

PROPELLER

Instead of the Hamilton Standard constant-speed propeller you used in the AT-6, you now use a 3-bladed Curtiss Electric propeller. To maintain a constant engine speed, the angle of the blades in the Curtiss Electric is varied through an arc of 30° (from 24.5° to 54.5°) by a propeller governor and electric motor. The current for operating the propeller governor and the electric motor comes **from** the battery and generator **through** propeller switches on the cockpit switch panel **to** the propeller control system.

You can operate the propeller automatically or manually. For all ordinary purposes you use automatic operation. Manual, or FIXED PITCH, operation is for emergencies.

When you operate the propeller automatically, the desired engine speed is held constant by a governor which is set by the propeller control on the throttle quadrant.

When you operate it manually, the blade angle is varied by means of a dashboard selector switch which is independent of the governor.

PROPELLER CONTROL

The propeller is controlled by a breaker switch and a selector switch.

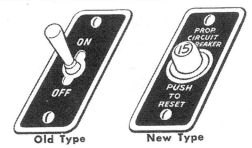

Old Type   New Type

1. BREAKER SWITCH

The breaker switch is an overload switch with ON and OFF positions. For all normal operations, use the ON position. When there is an overload current on the propeller's electrical system, the breaker switch snaps to OFF. Should this happen, put the selector switch in FIXED PITCH. Wait 15 seconds and push the breaker switch back to ON.

Note: When the breaker switch goes to OFF during takeoff, don't wait. Push it back to ON immediately.

There are two types of breaker switches. The new type is a pop-out switch resembling a cigar lighter on an automobile dashboard. When it is out, its red base is visible. Push it back to put it in the ON position. The old-type switch looks and works like an electric light switch.

2. SELECTOR SWITCH

The selector switch has four positions:

A. AUTO CONSTANT SPEED

When the switch is in this position, constant engine speed is maintained and the propeller blade angle is automatically varied by the propeller governor.

This is your normal operating position.

B. FIXED PITCH

With the switch in this position the electrical circuits of the propeller are open and the propeller operates as a fixed-pitch propeller.

C. INC RPM   D. DEC RPM

To vary the angle of the blades when the propeller is in FIXED PITCH, move the selector switch to INC RPM or to DEC RPM and hold it there until desired rpm is reached. When you release it, it snaps back to FIXED PITCH. The INC RPM and DEC RPM positions are your only means of varying blade angle when the propeller is in FIXED PITCH. When the propeller is in AUTO CONSTANT SPEED you use the propeller control lever on the throttle quadrant to increase or decrease rpm. (On P-40 N's with prop and throttle linkage, you increase or decrease rpm by advancing or retarding the throttle.)

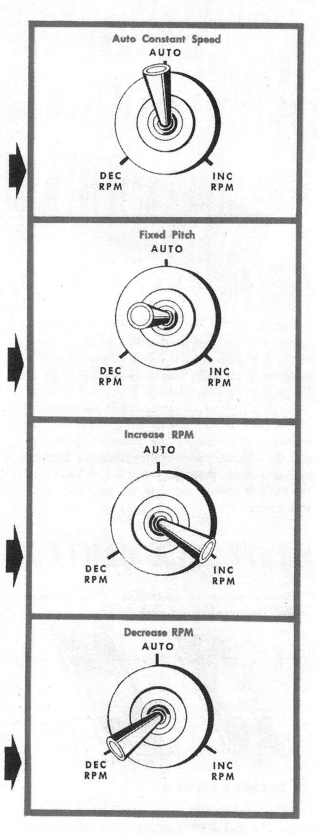

PROPELLER TROUBLE

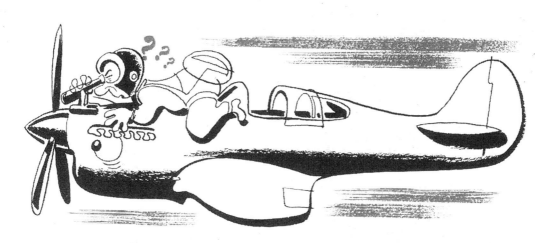

If the propeller goes out, whether through propeller or electrical system failure, it is likely to go to either maximum high or maximum low rpm. Here's what you do:

1. Move the propeller selector switch from the AUTO CONSTANT SPEED to the FIXED PITCH position.

2. Make sure the breaker switch is on.

3. Try to increase or decrease your rpm (whichever is needed) by moving the selector switch to the INC RPM or DEC RPM position.

4. If you can't adjust the rpm immediately, re-set the manifold pressure to the minimum that maintains flight, and land at the nearest field.

Caution

If the generator is out, cut off radio and all electrical circuits not needed. Then before you land, put the propeller breaker switch on and try to increase or decrease rpm to 2600 with a manifold pressure of 35" Hg.

If the tachometer oscillates while the propeller is in AUTO CONSTANT SPEED, move the selector switch to the FIXED PITCH position to find out what's wrong. If the oscillation continues while the propeller is in FIXED PITCH, you know that the trouble is either in the engine or instruments. If the oscillation stops, the trouble is in the propeller or propeller controls. Make the proper entry in your Form 1A.

ELECTRICAL SYSTEM

A 24-volt battery and a generator supply power for the propeller, fuel gage, hydraulic system, starter, radio equipment, needle and ball (if electric), guns, and gunsight, and all instrument, landing, and navigation lights.

AMMETER

The ammeter is to the left of or below the circuit breaker switches and ranges from 0 to 150 amps. After flying for a while, the ammeter should normally charge about 10 amps. When you are moving wheels or flaps up or down, it indicates from 40 to 75 amps, depending on the charge in the battery.

If the ammeter shows no current during flight, or if it continues to charge 50 amps or more, for more than 15 minutes after takeoff, the generator has failed. Follow this procedure:

1. Place the propeller switch in FIXED PITCH.

2. Cut all electrical switches.

3. Return to your field immediately for a landing. Extend your landing gear and flaps with the hand hydraulic pump. This conserves battery power needed for governing the propeller. It takes 175 to 200 strokes on the hand pump to extend the landing gear.

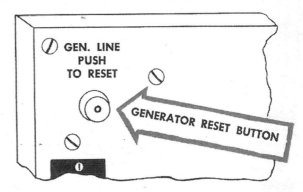

NOTE:

Early models of the P-40 N have a red pop-out type generator re-set button beneath the throttle quadrant. This button pops out when a generator overload breaks the connection between generator and battery. To re-set the generator, push the button in. Don't hold it in if it is trying to pop out. Push it in and take your hand off. If it persists in popping out, cut off the generator switch and return to the field and land.

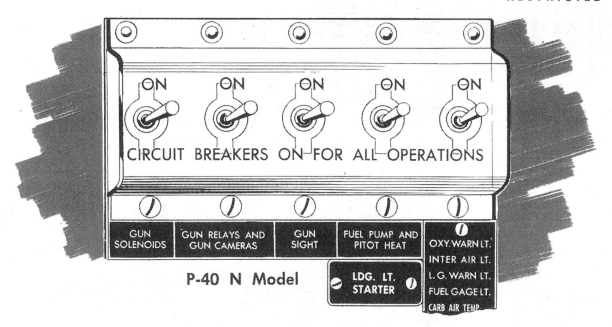

P-40 N Model

ELECTRIC BREAKER SWITCHES

The P-40's breaker switches, on the right side of the instrument switchboard, are of two types: ARMAMENT (on the left) and MISCELLANEOUS (on the right). The N model has two MISCELLANEOUS switches; all other models have three. Turn on the MISCELLANEOUS switches for all engine operations.

The ARMAMENT switches must be used when firing and must be off at all other times. Starting from the left, the first three breaker switches control the guns and the fourth controls the gunsight. (The P-40 N has only three ARMAMENT breaker switches—the first two for guns, the third for the gunsight.)

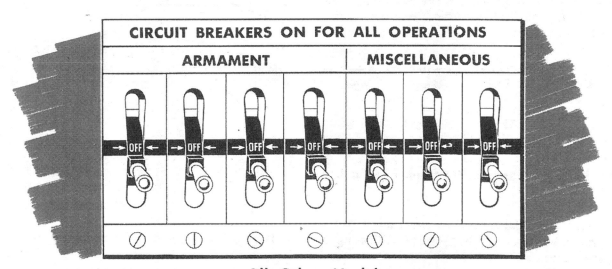

All Other Models

FUEL SYSTEM

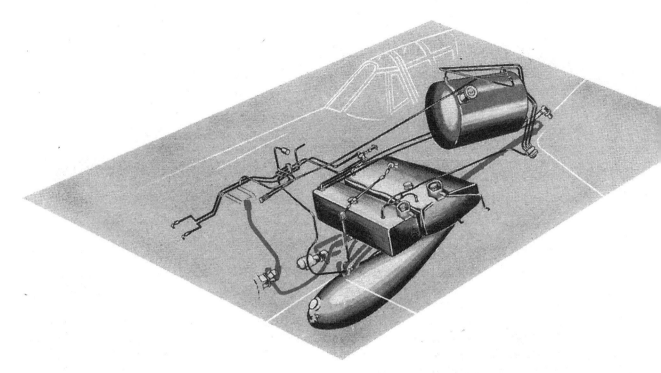

All P-40's (except a few early P-40 N's) contain a front wing tank, main wing tank and fuselage tank. Tank capacities are shown in the following table:

P-40 M and earlier models	Front Wing	Main Wing	Fuselage
P-40 M and earlier models	35 gal.	50.5 gal.	62.5 gal.
P-40 N	35 gal.	54 gal.	68 gal.

At the normal fuel consumption of 50 to 60 gallons per hour you have about 2½ hours of safe operation in a P-40.

Note: Formation flying, in which power settings constantly change, greatly increases your fuel consumption.

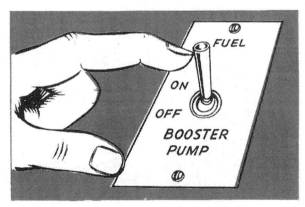

A belly tank, varying from 52 to 150 gallons in capacity, can be installed for additional range.

The fuel is carried to your engine by an engine-driven fuel pump and/or an electric booster pump. When starting the engine, and for all normal operations, the electric booster pump should be ON.

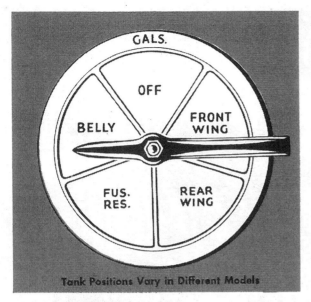

Tank Positions Vary in Different Models

FUEL SELECTOR VALVE

You change tanks by means of a fuel selector valve forward of the throttle quadrant. Turn the selector from one tank to the next until you feel it click into position. Be sure you feel the click; it insures that the proper selection is made. Arrange the sequence of tank changes so that you always change directly from an empty tank to a full one without passing the selector through another empty tank. Remember, the selector moves in both directions. When you pass through an empty tank to get to a full one you run the risk of getting a vapor lock.

Caution: Never pass the selector through the belly tank position when there is no belly tank installed.

Unless absolutely necessary, don't run any tank lower than 5 gallons indicated.

Maintain your fuel pressure between 16 and 18 psi. When the pressure falls below 10 psi, a red warning light on the left side of the dashboard flashes on (except on P-40 N which has no light). Don't hesitate when you see that red light. Change tanks immediately.

VENTED TANK

The fuselage tank is called the vented tank, which means that there is an overflow fuel line between this tank and the carburetor. The fuel line carries excess gas from the carburetor back to the fuselage tank. At high engine rpm, the fuel overflow may run as high as 10 or 15 gallons per hour.

Always use the fuselage tank for takeoff. During takeoff the chance of fuel overflow is especially high, and unless you are using the fuselage tank—the only one built to handle overflow gas—the overflow is lost.

After takeoff, always use at least 15 gallons from the fuselage tank before switching to another fuel tank.

The fuselage tank accumulates possible overflows from the other tanks during flight. Always turn the selector handle to the fuselage tank if it appears that you have run out of gas. The fuselage tank probably contains a few gallons of overflow fuel.

FUEL GAGE

There is an electrically operated fuel gage for the fuselage tank on the instrument panel. Direct reading gages for wing tanks are on the floor of the cockpit.

The P-40 normally uses Grade 100 fuel. When fuel of a lower grade is used, a **red tag** is prominently displayed in the cockpit.

OIL SYSTEM

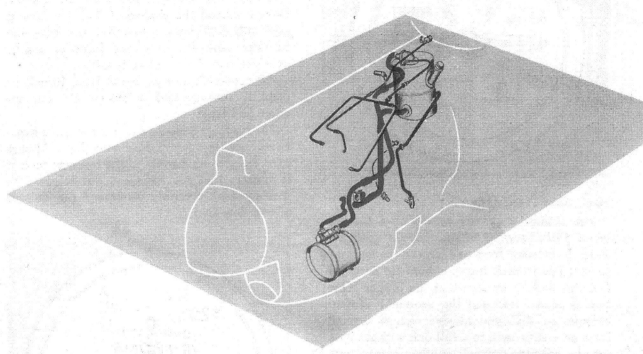

The oil tank capacity of the P-40 N is 8 gallons. In the K and M models it is 12.9 gallons. Following is a table of weights of oil used:

Cold weather:	AN 1080	SAE 77
Temperate weather:	1100	98
Hot weather:	1120	120

OIL PRESSURE AND TEMPERATURE GAGE

An engine-driven pump forces the oil from a storage tank to the engine at a pressure of from 60 to 80 psi. On the way back from the engine to the tank, the oil is cooled by a radiator which is regulated by manually operated shutters. These shutters also control coolant temperature.

Oil pressure and oil temperature are shown on a gage on the right side of the instrument panel. For normal operation, the oil pressure should be between 60 and 80 psi, temperature between 60° and 80° (maximum 95°).

passes through the filler neck of the oil tank. If the engine is cold, fill the tank to about 3 inches below the rivet; if the engine is hot, fill the tank right up to the rivet.

Never attempt climbs of 60° or more, or dives of 90°, unless your oil tank is filled to at least ⅓ of maximum capacity.

OIL OVERHEATING

If the oil temperature rises above 85° when you are cruising, open the coolant shutters all the way, reduce the power, and dive the airplane slightly.

OIL DILUTION SWITCH

There is an oil dilution switch on the instrument panel on all models up to the N. On the N it is below and to the right of the instrument panel. When outside temperature is below freezing, dilute the oil before stopping the engine. Run the engine at 1000 rpm and hold the dilution switch ON for at least 4 minutes or until the oil pressure drops to 15 psi. Do not dilute unless the oil temperature is below 50°.

Fill the oil tank by removing the fuselage cover between the firewall and the windshield. The oil level is determined by a rivet that

Caution:

Don't dive faster than 250 mph with your shutters open. Return to the field and land if the temperature stays high.

If the oil overheats when you are climbing, open the cowl shutters and level off. Reduce the power and start a slight dive with the shutters open. If that does not help, go back to the field and land.

COOLANT SYSTEM

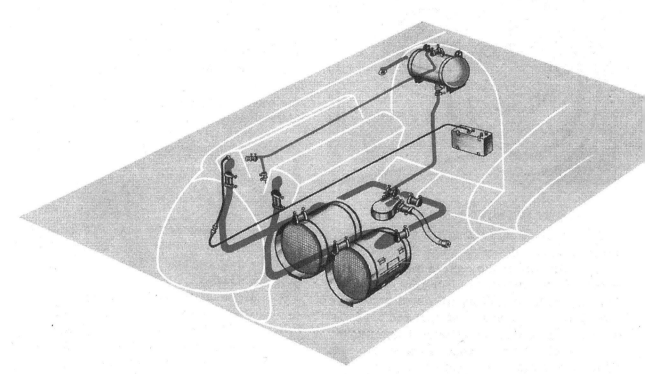

An engine-driven pump circulates the ethyline glycol coolant through the engine and back to the radiators. The coolant tank capacity is 3.7 gallons. The tank is filled through a filler neck forward of the windshield on top of the engine cowl.

You regulate the coolant temperature manually by opening and closing the cowl shutters. For normal ground operations, on takeoff and on landing, the shutters should be in FULL OPEN. When climbing and cruising, adjust the shutters to maintain a temperature of 85° to 125°. The desired temperature is between 95° and 105°.

COOLANT TEMPERATURE GAGE

The coolant temperature gage is on the right side of the instrument panel and is graded from —50° to 150°. On all models except the N a warning light flashes on when the coolant temperature reaches 125°.

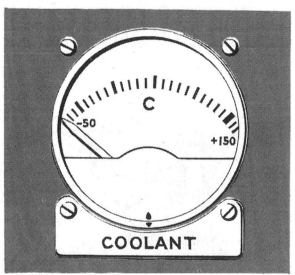

Whenever the coolant temperature reacnes 115° during cruising or 125° while climbing, follow the procedures for oil overheating described in the preceding section.

HYDRAULIC SYSTEM

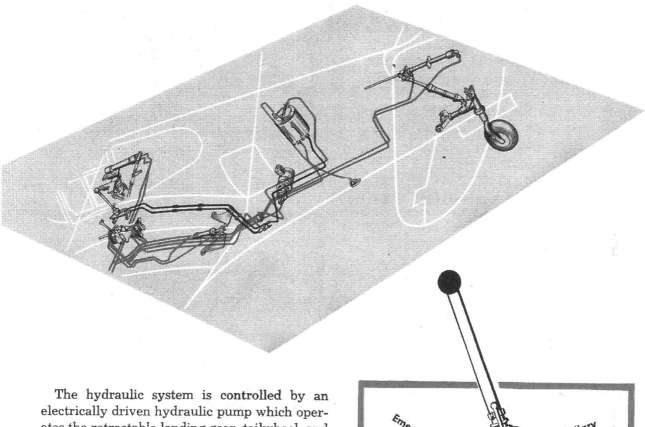

The hydraulic system is controlled by an electrically driven hydraulic pump which operates the retractable landing gear, tailwheel, and flaps. There is a hand-operated hydraulic pump attached to the floor of the cockpit on the right side. On models through the P-40 L, there is an additional hand-operated hydraulic pump inboard of the main hydraulic pump. This is an **emergency** pump, not an auxiliary pump. **Use it only in an emergency.** Operate by removing pump handle from regular, or outboard, pump and attaching it to the emergency, or inboard, pump.

To check the functioning of the hydraulic system on the ground:

1. Place the flap handle DOWN. This allows the flaps to drop 10° to 15°.

2. Put the flap handle in UP and pump up the flaps with the hand hydraulic pump until you build up a solid pressure.

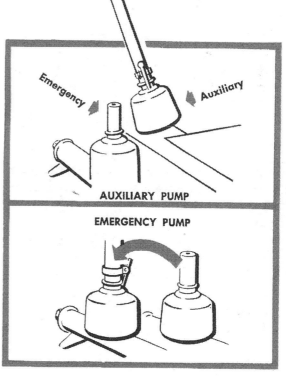

Emergency   Auxiliary

AUXILIARY PUMP

EMERGENCY PUMP

LANDING GEAR

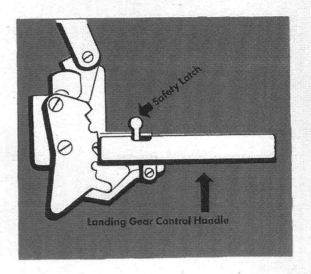

The hydraulically operated landing gear is controlled by a selector handle on the left side of the cockpit. The selector handle has three positions: UP, NEUTRAL, DOWN. To prevent accidental movement of the selector handle while the airplane is on the ground, there is a small locking pin on top of the handle. You don't have to release the pin to move the handle DOWN, but you must push it forward before you can move the handle to the UP position. The lock re-engages when you place the selector handle in NEUTRAL.

TO RETRACT THE LANDING GEAR

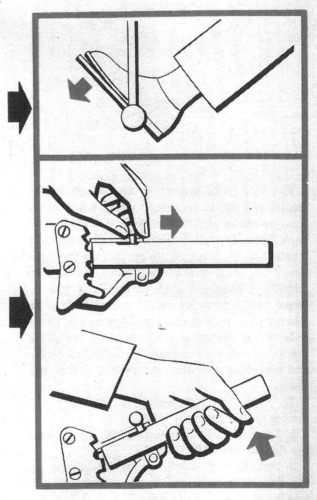

1. Apply pressure to brake the wheels.

2. Move the locking pin on the selector handle forward and place the selector handle in the UP position.

3. Depress the toggle switch on the control stick.

4. Observe the movement of the wheel indicators. It requires approximately 20 seconds to retract the wheels completely. When the wheels are fully retracted you can usually hear a high-pitched whine through the headset.

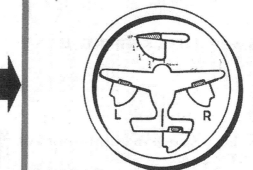

5. Try to move the hydraulic hand pump backward and forward when the indicators show the landing gear is fully retracted. If the wheels are all the way up, you won't be able to move the hand pump after a few strokes. Continue the action with the hand pump until it won't move.

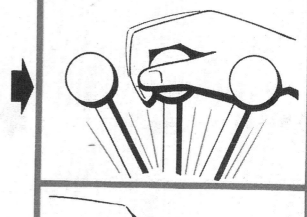

6. Return the selector handle to NEUTRAL.

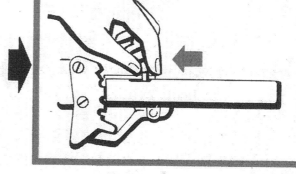

TO LOWER THE LANDING GEAR

1. Slow the airplane to an indicated airspeed (IAS) of 175 mph or less.

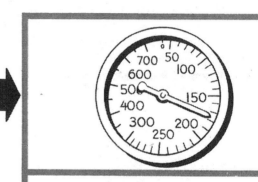

2. Move the selector handle to DOWN.

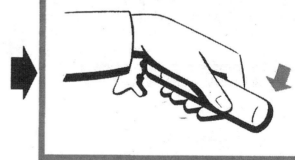

3. Depress the toggle switch on the stick.

4. Observe the movement of the indicators. It requires approximately 20 seconds to extend the wheels.

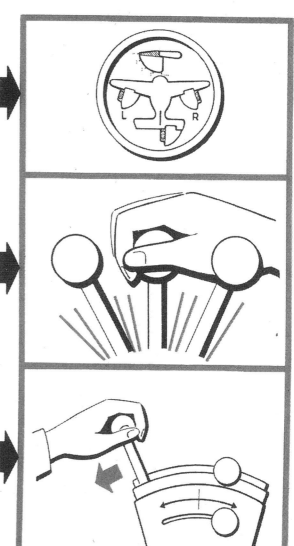

5. When movement of the indicators ceases, leave the handle in the DOWN position, and **check the hand hydraulic pump for stiffness.** Be sure that you check the hand pump both backward and forward. Be sure, also, that you leave the handle in the DOWN position while making this check.

6. Momentarily retard the throttle to see that the horn does not blow (if warning horn is installed.) **Remember that your hand hydraulic pump is the only accurate check you have.** The horn may be out, the indicators out, and other checks may be inaccurate, but if the hand hydraulic pump can't be moved after a stroke or two, you know that your wheels are down and locked.

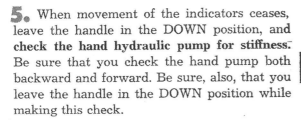

NOTE: Do not move selector handle up past the NEUTRAL position while on the ground, because the tailwheel retracts.

MANUAL OPERATION

You can extend or retract the gear if the electric motor fails by pumping with the hand hydraulic pump. Approximately 175 to 200 full strokes are necessary.

EMERGENCY OPERATION

If electric **and manual** operations fail and your airplane has the emergency hydraulic system, you extend the main landing gear as follows:

1. Move the selector handle DOWN.

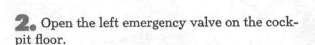

2. Open the left emergency valve on the cockpit floor.

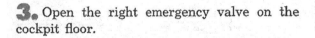

3. Open the right emergency valve on the cockpit floor.

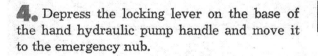

4. Depress the locking lever on the base of the hand hydraulic pump handle and move it to the emergency nub.

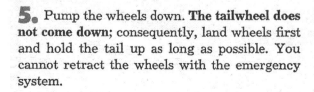

5. Pump the wheels down. **The tailwheel does not come down**; consequently, land wheels first and hold the tail up as long as possible. You cannot retract the wheels with the emergency system.

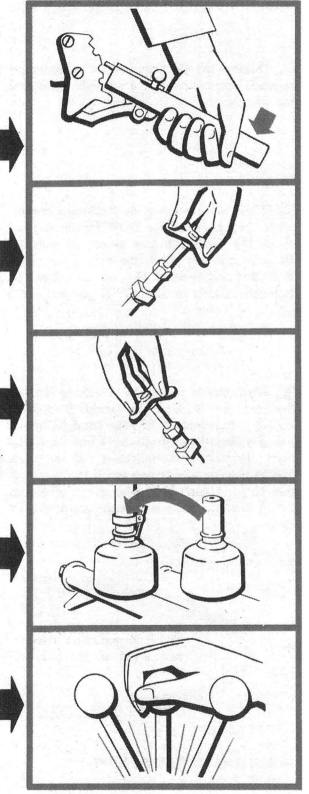

WHEEL INDICATORS

On all models except L, N, and late M's, there is an electric wheel and flap indicator on the instrument panel. Three tabs in the indicator show the relative position of the main landing gear and the tailwheel. (A pointer indicator shows the position of the flaps.)

The wheel indicator on the L, N, and late M's is a yellow peg which rises directly above the oleo strut hinge on both right and left main wheels when the gear is down. The peg rises as the wheel extends, and it goes down when the wheel retracts.

FLAPS

The flap controls have three positions—DOWN, NEUTRAL, and UP. The flaps are operated hydraulically by an electric toggle switch on the forward side of the stick. When you want to move your flaps up or down, put the flap control into the UP or DOWN position and depress the toggle switch. (You can also operate them manually by using the hand hydraulic pump.)

You can lower the flaps to an angle of 45° or stop them at any point before 45°.

The L, N, and late M models have peg flap indicators. The indicator peg rises from the trailing edge of the wing. The peg is fully extended from the wing when the flaps are full down. Colored bands indicate the degree of extension of the flaps in this manner:

Yellow . . . . .15°
Yellow and green .30°
Green and red . . . . .45°

The position of the flaps on all other P-40 models is shown by a pointer on the wheel and flap indicator on the instrument panel.

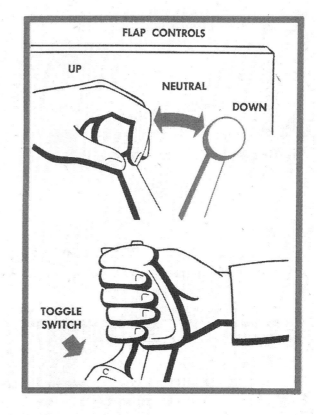

FLAP CONTROLS

UP NEUTRAL DOWN

TOGGLE SWITCH

BRAKES

The brakes are single-shoe expansion type, hydraulically operated. The usual toe action on the rudder pedals controls each brake independently.

Test your brakes when you taxi out to the takeoff position. If either brake is soft, return to the line.

Never apply brakes suddenly; you may nose up the airplane. Take it easy on your brakes when you taxi. Don't ride them. Riding makes them heat rapidly, and the heat may glaze the brake drum. Control the airplane with the steerable tailwheel as much as possible. If either or both brakes fail, stop the airplane by cutting off the engine immediately.

PARKING BRAKE HANDLE

The parking brake handle is on the left-hand side of the instrument panel.

To set the brakes:

1. Depress the rudder brake pedals.

2. Pull the parking brake handle out.

3. Release the pedal pressure.

4. Release the parking brake handle.

To release the parking brakes, simply push down on the rudder brake pedals.

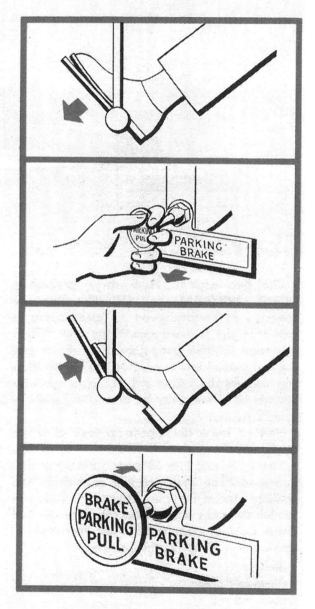

Caution: Never set the parking brake when the brakes are hot. The brakes may lock. Never set the parking brake in flight.

RADIO

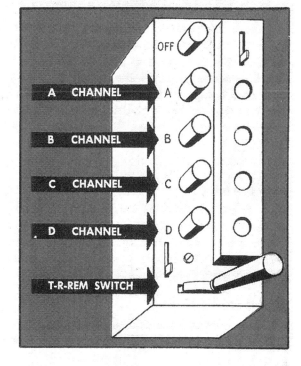

Two kinds of radio are used in the P-40—the VHF 522-A and the SCR 274-N. The VHF is a very high frequency radio; the 274-N is a long-range radio that can receive high, medium and low frequencies.

VHF

The VHF has a push button control with an OFF position and four channels for transmitting and receiving. The radio is on when one of the channel buttons is pushed in.

A Channel is for squadron interplane communication.

B Channel is the all-American common frequency. You can contact all radio towers using VHF on B Channel, and you can also use it for emergency homings.

C and **D Channels** are generally used for local tower and local homing station frequencies.

TO TRANSMIT ON THE VHF SET:

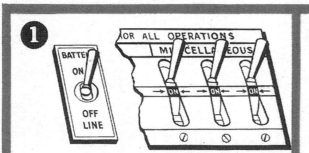

1 Put battery switch and circuit breakers in the ON position.

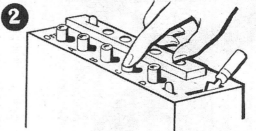

2 Place the T-R-REM (Transmit, Receive and Remote) switch in position REM. This switch is normally safetied in REM.

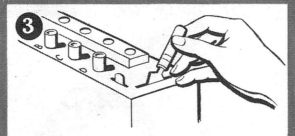

3 Press the button of the channel you want. Allow about one minute for the tubes to warm up.

4 Press the press-to-talk button on the throttle and talk.

Note: If the press-to-talk button isn't working, you can transmit by placing the T-R-REM switch in the T position. If you use the T position, be sure not to leave the switch in T after you are through talking. If you do, you can't receive and you block out anybody trying to transmit in your vicinity. Whenever you use the T, put the switch into the R position as soon as you finish transmitting, so you can receive.

TO RECEIVE

To receive on the VHF set, release the press-to-talk button and adjust volume with the dial on the side of the control box. To receive when the press-to-talk button isn't working, place the T-R-REM switch in R.

DETROLA

Planes having VHF radios also have a Detrola, a low-frequency (200-400 Kc) receiver,

on the floor of the cockpit. Use the Detrola to receive control towers, radio beams and range stations transmitting on low frequencies. To operate, switch it on and tune to the frequency you want. You can receive over both VHF and Detrola at the same time. The Detrola has no transmitter.

SCR 274-N

The 274-N set comprises a receiver box, transmitter box, and filter switch box control.

RECEIVER BOX

The receiver box has three dials, one for each of the three separate receiver units. The

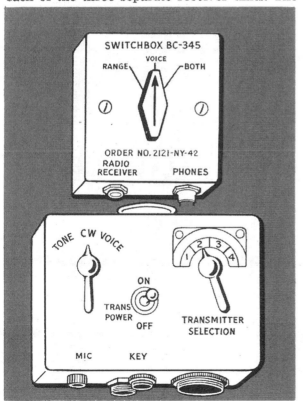

first dial is set for 3 to 6 Mc; the second for 190 to 550 Kc; the third for 6 to 9.1 Mc.

Above and to the left of each dial is a selector switch for A and B receiver channels. This switch is normally in A.

Above and to the right of each dial there is a battery switch with three positions: CW (code), OFF, and MCW (voice). This switch is ordinarily in the MCW position for receiving voice.

Below and to the right of each dial is a small tuning crank which turns the dial. Below and to the left is the volume control.

FILTER SWITCH BOX

The filter switch box must be used in conjunction with the receiver boxes. It has three positions: RANGE, VOICE, or BOTH.

TRANSMITTER BOX

The transmitter box has controls for four transmitting frequencies. The P-40 usually carries two transmitters, only one of which can be used at a time. The transmitters are pre-set on different frequencies which are recorded in the write-in space on the control box.

The transmitter control box has a battery switch with OFF and ON positions; an emission switch with TONE, CW, and VOICE positions; a transmitter selector switch with which you choose the transmitter desired; and a key on top of the box to transmit code.

TO RECEIVE

1. Move receiver box switch from OFF to MCW (for voice) or CW (for code).

2. Place channel selector switch in A or B to correspond with the jack used for the headset plug. It is usually A.

3. Set filter box switch control to RANGE, VOICE or BOTH, whichever is desired.

4. Tune to frequency desired with the tuning knob.

5. Adjust volume with the volume control.

TO TRANSMIT

1. Move the transmitter selector switch to the transmitting frequency desired.

2. Set the battery switch ON. (Allow about 15 seconds to warm up the tubes.)

3. Place the emission switch on TONE, CW, or VOICE, as desired.

4. Press down the press-to-talk button on the stick and talk.

MICROPHONE

The VHF set and 274-N both employ a throat mike which fits over your vocal chords just below your chin. Adjust the mike by lengthening or shortening the elastic band which goes around the back of your neck. Keep the mike fitting snugly—about as tight as a necktie.

For best results when transmitting, press the mike firmly against your throat with your hand.

EMERGENCY PROCEDURE

If your radio is out, rock your wings upon approaching a landing field. At night blink your

landing lights. The tower flashes your landing instructions: green light means come in; red light means wait.

Caution: Do not lower your landing light if your airspeed is higher than 140 mph.

OXYGEN EQUIPMENT

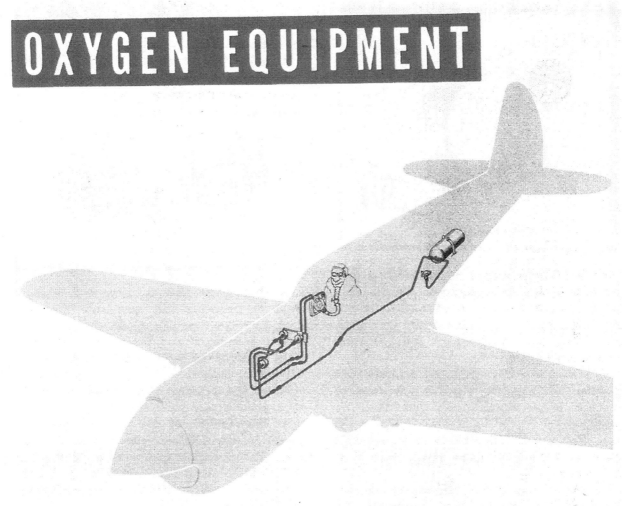

The P-40 has one of two types of oxygen systems—demand or constant flow. The demand type is the newer, improved system and it has been installed in as many airplanes as possible. Some of the older types, however, still use the constant flow system.

Your **Pilots' Information File** contains thorough discussions of both systems. If you haven't read it in your PIF yet, do so now. Know your oxygen equipment—your life depends upon it.

A few facts about the two systems follow:

DEMAND TYPE

1. Use it when or before you reach 10,000 feet indicated altitude. (On flights of 4 hours or more, begin using oxygen between 8000 and 10,000 feet.) Never wait until you are above 10,000 feet.

2. The rubber mask hose has a metal connector by which you attach it to the oxygen regulator. Make sure it is connected tightly. It slips out easily, so you have to keep checking the connection.

3. A low-pressure oxygen cylinder of 1000 cubic-inch capacity is in the fuselage baggage compartment. Refill the cylinder by attaching a master cylinder to the filler valve just inside the fuselage access door. Do not fill to pressures greater than 450 psi.

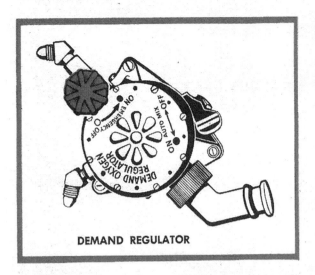

DEMAND REGULATOR

knurled knob on the side of the regulator. This gives you pure oxygen under **positive pressure** in a steady flow.

Caution: Use the red knob only in extreme emergencies, because it depletes your oxygen system in about 8 minutes.

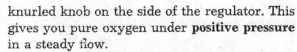

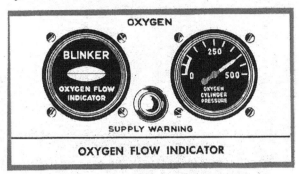

OXYGEN FLOW INDICATOR

4. The flow of oxygen to the mask is governed by a demand regulator on the right side of the cockpit. On the side of the regulator is an AUTO MIX lever with ON and OFF positions, and a red knurled knob that opens the emergency bypass.

5. With the AUTO MIX lever in the ON position, the regulator supplies a mixture of air and oxygen automatically determined by your needs.

6. With the AUTO MIX lever in the OFF position, you breathe pure oxygen each time you inhale.

7. The automatic regulator can be entirely bypassed by opening the emergency red

8. The oxygen flow indicator is a blinking light or bouncing ball type and blinks or bounces every time you inhale when the pressure is between 50 and 500 psi. As long as the light blinks or the ball bounces, you know you are getting oxygen.

Note: The indicator operates only when the emergency bypass valve is closed.

9. The duration of the oxygen supply depends on the individual pilot and on the altitude. The average is approximately 2 hours in AUTO MIX; about 1 hour in OFF (pure oxygen) and about 8 minutes when emergency knob is open.

CONSTANT FLOW

The constant flow system is the same as you used in the AT-6. Turn it on when or before you reach 10,000 feet. (8000-10,000 feet on flights of 4 hours or more.) Control the constant flow system manually by opening a valve on the oxygen gage on the right side of the cockpit. The gage is marked off in altitudes.

Caution: Always keep the indicator turned 5000 feet above your actual altitude. Be sure to check your mask bag for leaks before takeoff.

COCKPIT

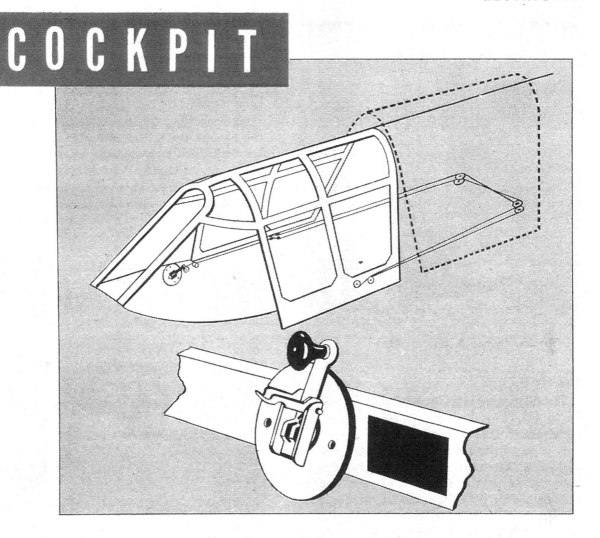

CANOPY

The cockpit is enclosed by a sliding plexiglas canopy and protected in front by a bullet-proof windshield.

The canopy is opened and shut by a crank handle on the right side of the cockpit. At the base of the crank is a locking lever. When the lever is depressed, a locking peg on the crank catches in one of three holes, locking the canopy in place. When the lever is out, the crank is free to turn. Always be sure the lever is out when you leave the cockpit. When the lever is out, you can open and shut the canopy by giving it a shove forward or backward from the outside.

The canopy has two emergency releases. One is above your head when the canopy is closed. This release disengages the whole canopy and allows the slipstream to carry it off during flight.

Note: When the canopy is tightly closed the slipstream sometimes fails to dislodge it. If this happens you can easily dump the canopy by giving it a slight push up or back.

The second emergency canopy release is on the left side of the canopy. This opens only the side panel. You can operate it from either inside or outside.

The canopy must be closed and locked during all aerobatics and maneuvers in which the speed exceeds cruising.

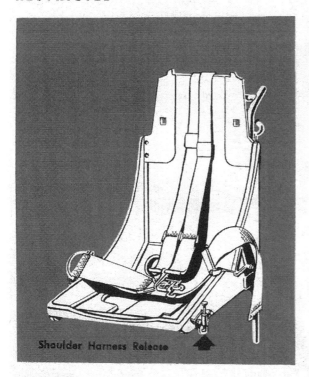

Shoulder Harness Release

SEATING

The pilot's seat in all models except the N can be raised or lowered by a small lever on the right side of the seat.

A safety belt and shoulder harness are attached to the back of the seat. Fasten the shoulder harness to the front of your belt by pulling it over your shoulders, suspender fashion, and hooking it to the clasp in the center of the belt. **Keep your harness and belt fastened at all times during flight.**

The shoulder harness has two positions— locked and unlocked. When it is unlocked you have freedom of movement in the seat (within the confines of your safety belt). To strap yourself firmly in the seat, lock the harness by pressing a small lever on the left side of the seat forward. **Your harness must be locked for all takeoffs, landings and aerobatics.** To unlock the harness, push the locking lever backward.

A fire extinguisher is under the seat, and a first-aid kit is attached to the side of the cockpit on the right side of the seat.

LIGHTING

Two movable spotlights, one on each side of the canopy tract, illuminate the cockpit. They are controlled by a rheostat on the instrument panel. In models up to and including the M, there is a movable fluorescent lamp on the left side next to the instrument panel. This is controlled by a rheostat next to the spotlight rheostat. There is a light in the compass for easy reading.

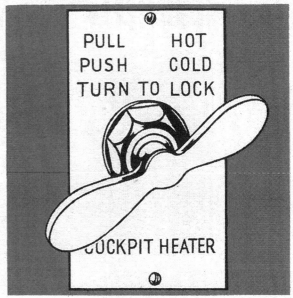

HEATING

The cockpit heat regulator, on the right side of the instrument panel, moves from FULL COLD to FULL HOT or stops at any point between the two. Release the spring-loaded handle by turning counter-clockwise, move to point desired, and re-lock by turning clockwise.

Pilot's Ground Checks

Before you get into your airplane, look it over closely. Walk around and inspect the wings, fuselage and control surfaces. Look carefully; take your time.

Before you climb into the cockpit be sure you have checked all of the following:

1. Check your tires and tailwheel. See that the struts have plenty of clearance. An instruction plate on each strut shows the necessary clearance.

2. Make sure the cover is off the pitot tube.

3. See that the covers are on the gun hatches.

4. See that the caps are fastened tightly on the gas, oil, and coolant tanks.

5. Make sure the Dzus fasteners are secure, and check the fairing on the entire ship for looseness.

6. Find out whether the propeller has been pulled through. It needs at least four turns if the engine is cold.

7. See that the wings and wingtips are not damaged.

8. Check canopy for proper tolerance.

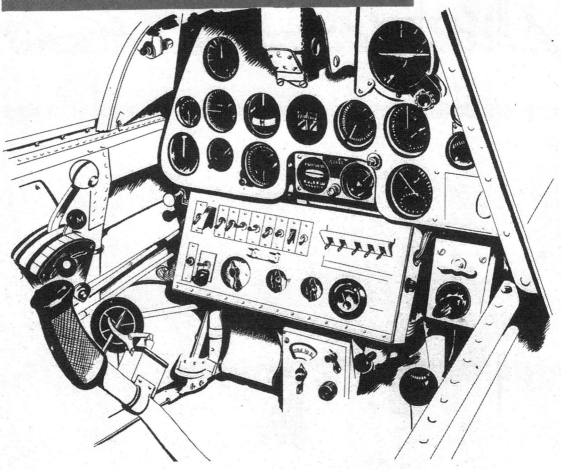

COCKPIT CHECK

The place to find out if there is anything wrong is on the ground.

After you are in the cockpit but before you start the engine, go through this procedure:

1. Check your Form 1A for servicing, pilot's remarks, and condition of the airplane. Question the crew chief about the airplane before you take off.

2. Adjust seat, safety belt, shoulder harness, and rudder pedals.

3. Check the throat mike, headset and radio. Adjust the mike to fit snugly around your neck.

4. See that the canopy emergency releases are locked.

5. Make the following left to right cockpit check:

   a. Flap handle—NEUTRAL.

   b. Landing gear—DOWN.

   c. Trim tabs—Rudder 2° right; elevator—T.O.

   d. Throttle quadrant—¼ open.

   e. Propeller switches—ON and AUTO.

   f. Oxygen pressure—not less than 350 psi. if you are making an altitude flight.

   g. Carburetor heat control—COLD.

   h. Coolant shutters—OPEN.

   i. Check fuel gages. (When the airplane is at rest, the wing tank gages show 10-15 gallons less than there actually is in the tank.)

STARTING

1. Set the coolant shutters in full OPEN.
2. Crack the throttle ¼ open.
3. Set mixture control in IDLE CUT-OFF.
4. Set the propeller control full forward; place the propeller switches in ON and AUTO.
5. Set carburetor air control in COLD.
6. Turn fuel selector to fuselage tank.
7. Call "Clear!" in a loud and distinct voice. Receive acknowledgement from the crew chief.
8. Turn ignition switch to BOTH.
9. Turn battery switch ON.

10. Turn on the three MISCELLANEOUS breaker switches. (On the P-40 N turn on the two right-hand breaker switches.)
11. Turn on the electric fuel booster pump.
12. Begin energizing the starter.
13. Prime the engine one stroke if warm, three strokes if cold.
14. Engage starter. When the engine starts firing, advance the mixture control to the AUTO RICH position.
15. Retard the throttle to idle at 1000 rpm.

THREE THINGS TO REMEMBER:

1. If the engine stops firing return the mixture control to IDLE CUT-OFF.

2. Never run the booster pump if the engine stops firing and the mixture control is **not** in IDLE CUT-OFF.

3. Stop the engine immediately if the oil pressure doesn't register at least 15 psi within 15 seconds.

OVERPRIMING

If the engine does not fire because of overpriming, **turn off all switches** and pull the propeller through two or three complete revolutions. When you start again, be extra careful not to overprime.

If flame comes out of the exhaust stacks while you are starting the engine, shut off the electric fuel booster pump, put the mixture control in IDLE CUT-OFF, open the throttle wide, and keep the engine turning over with the starter until the flames stop. If the engine should start with the throttle wide open, close the throttle immediately—before adjusting other controls.

STOPPING THE ENGINE

1. Apply brake treadles and set the parking brake.

2. Hold the stick back and run engine up to approximately 1300 rpm for 5 seconds.

3. Pull mixture control to IDLE CUT-OFF and slowly advance throttle to full open.

Note: If engine does not stop, return mixture control to AUTO RICH and idle at 1000 rpm until engine cools. Then repeat stopping procedures.

4. When the propeller stops rotating, turn the ignition switch to OFF. Turn generator, battery, breaker, and radio switches to OFF.

5. Call in a loud voice, "Switches off!"

6. Release brakes.

ENGINE WARM-UP and GROUND TEST

1. Start warming up the engine at 800-1000 rpm until the oil pressure remains steady at 60-70 psi.

2. When the oil pressure no longer fluctuates and the temperature begins to rise, gradually increase engine speed to 1400 rpm. The minimum oil temperature at 1400 rpm or over is 15°.

3. If icing conditions exist, move the carburetor air control to HOT.

4. Oil pressure should not exceed 120 psi during warm-up and oil temperature should be 60° to 80°, with maximum of 85°. Fuel pressure for idling should be 12 to 15 psi.

5. Avoid prolonged ground running of the engine. After warm-up has been completed, set propeller selector switch to FIXED PITCH and advance the throttle to 28" Hg. Move the propeller selector switch to INC RPM or DEC RPM to get 2200 rpm.

a. To test the magnetos and sparkplugs, move the ignition switch from BOTH to L, back to BOTH, then to R, and back to BOTH. The normal loss on one magneto should not exceed 80 rpm.

b. Check the fuel and oil pressure and oil and coolant temperature.

c. Return the propeller selector switch to AUTO and push the propeller control all the way forward.

d. Vary the engine speed from 2300 to 2000 rpm with the propeller control. The manifold pressure should not vary more than 1" Hg.

e. To test the automatic operation of the propeller, pull back on propeller control until tachometer shows a loss of 200 rpm. Note that the tachometer maintains the reduced setting. Return the propeller control to takeoff setting, noting that the original rpm is regained.

f. If the battery is fully charged the ammeter indicates no charge. Depress the landing gear toggle switch, and watch the ammeter—it should show a charge of at least 5 to 10 amps.

HOT WEATHER TIPS

1. Keep the carburetor control in full COLD position at all times.

2. Open the coolant shutters before starting and on the peel-off before landing. This procedure cools the engine so you can taxi longer after you land.

3. Don't start the engine until you are ready to taxi.

4. If the engine overheats, pull off to the side of the taxi strip (at least 200 feet from the runway in use), point the nose of your airplane into the wind and shut off the engine until it cools. It takes about 15 minutes to cool an overheated engine.

COLD WEATHER TIPS

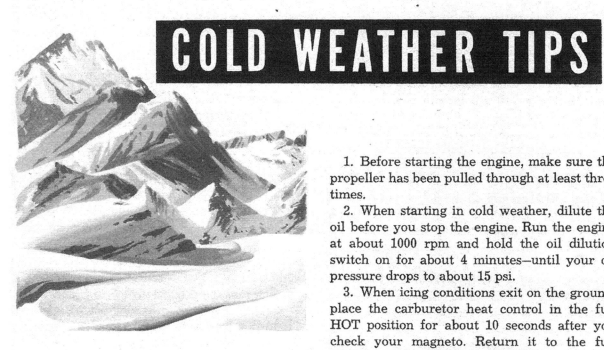

1. Before starting the engine, make sure the propeller has been pulled through at least three times.

2. When starting in cold weather, dilute the oil before you stop the engine. Run the engine at about 1000 rpm and hold the oil dilution switch on for about 4 minutes—until your oil pressure drops to about 15 psi.

3. When icing conditions exit on the ground, place the carburetor heat control in the full HOT position for about 10 seconds after you check your magneto. Return it to the full COLD position before the takeoff.

POWER SETTINGS

The following table of power settings is for operating the P-40 with Grade 100 fuel:

ALLISON ENGINE

GRADE 100 FUEL	MANIFOLD PRESSURE	ENGINE RPM
IDLING		1000
TAKEOFF (Maximum)	52" (for 1 minute)	3000
TAKEOFF (Recommended)	45" (for 5 minutes)	3000
CLIMB (Maximum)	45.5" (for 5 minutes)	2600
CLIMB (Recommended)	35"	2500
CRUISE (Maximum)	37.2"	2400
CRUISE (Recommended)	30"	2300
LANDING		2600

GRADE 100 FUEL	OIL PRESSURE	OIL TEMP.	FUEL PRESSURE	COOLANT TEMP.
MAXIMUM	85 psi	85°	18 psi	125°
MINIMUM	55 psi	60°	16 psi	85°
RECOMMENDED	60-70 psi	70°-80°	16-18 psi	95°-105°

Power Settings

ROLLS-ROYCE ENGINE

GRADE 100 FUEL	MANIFOLD PRESSURE	ENGINE RPM
IDLING		1000-1400
TAKEOFF (Maximum)	54" (for one minute)	3000
TAKEOFF (Recommended)	48" (for 5 minutes)	3000
CLIMB (Maximum)	48" (for 5 minutes)	2650
CLIMB (Recommended)	35"	2500
CRUISE (Maximum)	38"	2650
CRUISE (Recommended)	30"	2400
LANDING		2650

GRADE 100 FUEL	OIL PRESSURE	OIL TEMP.	FUEL PRESSURE	COOLANT TEMP.
MAXIMUM	90 psi	90°	16 psi	121°
MINIMUM	60 psi	40°	12 psi	60°
RECOMMENDED	70-80 psi	70°-80°	12-16 psi	95°

GRADE 91 FUEL

The great demands of the overseas air forces have often left domestic AAF stations without a sufficient supply of Grade 100 gasoline. Consequently, Grade 91 gasoline has been widely used at U.S. bases, particularly for training flights. With the tempo of war increasing, Grade 91 fuel will continue to be used.

The P-40 is a perfectly safe airplane to fly with Grade 91 gas. With a thorough knowledge of its operating limits, flying with Grade 91 should give you no trouble at all.

Remember, never use FULL RICH mixture control setting except in extreme emergencies when using Grade 91 gas.

Following are charts of power settings for the P-40 with Grade 91 fuel:

ALLISON ENGINE

GRADE 91 FUEL	MANIFOLD PRESSURE	ENGINE RPM
TAKEOFF (Maximum)	47"	3000
TAKEOFF (Recommended)	40"	3000
CLIMB (Maximum)	35"	2600
CLIMB (Recommended)	33"	2500
CRUISE (Maximum)	30"	2400
CRUISE (Recommended)	28"	2300
LANDING		2600

ROLLS-ROYCE ENGINE

GRADE 91 FUEL	MANIFOLD PRESSURE	ENGINE RPM
TAKEOFF (Maximum)	44.2"	3000
TAKEOFF (Recommended)	40"	3000
CLIMB (Maximum)	36"	2650
CLIMB (Recommended)	34"	2500
CRUISE (Maximum)	31"	2400
CRUISE (Recommended)	29"	2320
LANDING		2650

Flight Characteristics

The P-40 is a conventional modern fighting plane. It has no bugs and no tricky, unusual, or undesirable characteristics in takeoff, landing and flight.

Remember, it's not a trainer. It's fast, powerful, and responds quickly to controls. It's a combat airplane, which means it was designed as a flying gun platform. Consequently, it was made highly maneuverable. **For a fighter,** it's very stable in flight, but its stability depends on you. You must fly the airplane every second, from the time you start until you cut the engine off after landing. You cannot doze at the controls of a P-40.

TAXIING

1. Be sure the chocks have been removed and that there are no obstructions in front of you.

2. Use only enough power to start rolling.

3. Keep your canopy open.

4. Look out both sides, behind, and in front.

5. Taxi slowly, and when you taxi in a congested zone around the parking area, have someone at your wingtip.

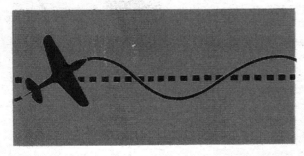

6. S continuously. Use steerable tailwheel as much as possible.

7. Brake intermittently; don't ride your brakes.

8. Hold the stick well back.

9. Keep both hands and feet on the proper controls.

10. Taxi at the minimum throttle setting—not under 1000 rpm.

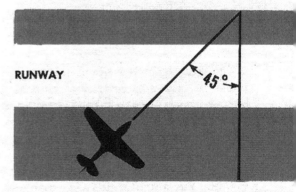

11. For the pre-takeoff check, stop off the runway at an angle of about 45° to the runway so that rear and forward vision of the runway is unobstructed.

12. Test brakes while taxiing out. If one or both brakes are weak, return to the line.

PRE-TAKEOFF CHECK

Make the following left-to-right check.

1. Canopy open.

2. Controls free.

3. Wing flaps up (unless needed and then never more than ½ down).

4. Trim tabs at takeoff setting—rudder 2° right; elevator T.O. (Electric aileron trim tab—neutral.)

5. Tighten friction knob on the throttle quadrant so that throttle and prop controls do not creep.

6. Propeller lever set full forward.

7. Mixture control—AUTO RICH.

8. Fuel cock on **vented** (fuselage) tank.

9. Propeller switches ON and AUTO CONSTANT SPEED.

10. Electric booster pump ON.

11. Battery and generator switches ON.

12. Oil pressure 60-80 psi; oil temperature 60° minimum, 85° maximum.

13. Fuel pressure 12-16 psi.

14. Coolant temperature 85° minimum, 125° maximum.

15. Engine primer OFF.

16. Carburetor air COLD.

17. Coolant shutters OPEN.

18. Check functioning of instruments, generator and magneto at 2300 rpm and 28″ Hg. Maximum drop on either magneto—80 rpm. If the engine cuts out or runs roughly on either magneto, return to the line.

At 30″ Hg. the ammeter should show a charge of at least 10 amps. (The generator cuts in at 1600-1700 rpm.) If the ammeter shows no charge going to the battery, depress the landing gear toggle switch and check the ammeter for generator charge. If the ammeter still shows no charge, return to the line.

19. Propeller check:

For all models except those N's with prop and throttle linkage, at 2300 rpm pull the propeller control lever back until the tachometer shows a drop of 200 rpm. Then return the control lever to the full forward position. Make sure the engine regains the original rpm setting.

To check manual operation of the propeller, place the propeller switch in FIXED PITCH, move to DEC RPM until the tachometer shows a 200 rpm drop; then place the propeller switch in the INC RPM position until the tachometer shows that the original rpm has been regained. Then return the propeller switch to the AUTO position.

For N models with prop and throttle linkage, put the propeller switch in the DEC RPM position, decrease by 200 rpm and return to AUTO. Watch the tachometer to see that the original rpm is regained. **Caution:** Be sure you return the propeller switch to AUTO.

TAKEOFF

Your takeoff in the P-40, except for greater torque, is not much different from that in the AT-6.

Apply power smoothly, because a sudden burst of power might make your airplane turn strongly to the left. Even with smooth application of power the airplane tends to swing to the left. Compensate for this tendency with firm use of right rudder.

Don't force the tail up violently in the early stages of the takeoff run. This makes you lose the use of the steerable tailwheel before you gain rudder control. During takeoff, torque tends to make the left wing drop; compensate with right aileron.

Follow this takeoff procedure:

1. Select a reference point on the horizon that you can keep clearly in sight during the takeoff.

2. Move the throttle forward steadily and evenly to 45″ Hg. (40″ Hg. for Grade 91). Don't joggle the throttle. Keep your hand on the throttle until you are well in the air.

3. As soon as you have sufficient speed, get the tail up **slightly**. Don't take off in a 3-point position.

4. Keep the airplane going straight down the runway by use of the rudder alone. Use brakes only in emergency.

5. Allow the airplane to fly itself off the ground with smooth back pressure on the stick.

6. Brake wheels and raise the landing gear as soon as you cannot make a wheels-down landing on the remainder of the runway. Adjust the trim tabs to ease pressure on the controls. As soon as the wheels are up and locked, check with the hand hydraulic pump and return the landing gear selector handle to NEUTRAL.

7. Reduce the throttle to 35″ Hg. (33″ Hg. for Grade 91 fuel) and 2500 rpm for climbing as soon as you are definitely airborne.

Note: If the flaps are used for takeoff, don't raise them until you have reached 500 feet.

AFTER TAKEOFF

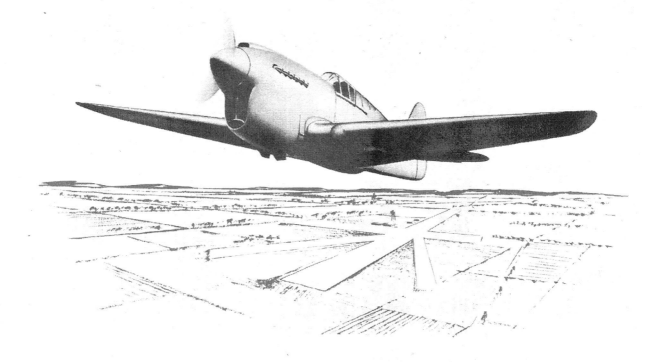

1. After takeoff reduce the throttle and rpm settings to 35″ Hg. (33″ Hg. for Grade 91) and 2500 rpm. Climb straight ahead at 150 mph IAS until you reach at least 300 feet altitude.

2. Adjust trim tabs so that there is little pressure on the controls.

3. Make your turn out of traffic and continue climbing at 150 to 160 mph IAS to the desired altitude.

4. S constantly while climbing. Keep a sharp lookout for other aircraft.

5. Check functioning of engine instruments frequently. If there is anything wrong, return to the field and land.

6. Coolant and oil temperatures generally run higher than normal while climbing. If either temperature persists in running abnormally high, level off until it drops.

7. When the desired altitude is reached, level off, and reduce throttle to 30″ Hg. (28″ Hg. for Grade 91) and approximately 2300 rpm for cruising.

8. Adjust coolant shutters and re-trim the airplane so that it flies straight ahead with your hands off the controls.

9. Keep checking instruments. Engine instruments and fuel gages should be checked at least once every 5 minutes.

LANDINGS

You have been used to flying a rectangular pattern. Now, with few exceptions, you have to fly a circular pattern, varying at different fields but generally to the left.

As you approach the field, tune your radio to the control tower frequency and turn the volume up. When you have received permission from the control tower to enter the pattern and are waiting for landing instructions, follow this procedure:

1. Circle the field at your assigned altitude (not under 1000 feet). Remember, there may be other planes in the pattern, some much slower than your P-40. While you maintain a constant turn, keep a sharp lookout on both sides, above, behind, and in front. Circle around the boundaries of the field, staying close enough to the field and keeping enough altitude to make an emergency landing from any position.

2. While circling make the following pre-landing check:

    a. Mixture control AUTO RICH.

    b. Engine 2600 rpm.

    c. Fuel selector valve on the fullest tank.

    d. Propeller switches ON and AUTO.

    e. Coolant shutters adjusted to keep coolant temperature under 105°.

    f. Shoulder harness locked.

3. After the tower gives you landing instructions and clearance to approach the field for a peel-off, slow to 170 mph and extend your landing gear.

4. Lock your canopy open.

5. Open your coolant shutters.

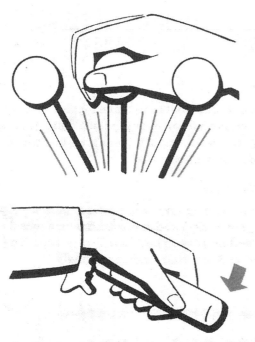

6. Check the landing gear **with the hand hydraulic pump. Landing gear handle must be in DOWN position.**

7. When the check is completed call "Wheels down and locked—Landing" to the control tower.

8. Re-trim the airplane.

9. Make the last turn into the field at an altitude of not less than 500 feet and a distance of not more than ¼ mile from the end of the runway. Get squared away with the runway.

10. Lower your flaps below 140 mph IAS.

11. Establish a glide of 110-115 mph and re-trim the airplane. It is usually a good idea to trim the airplane slightly tail-heavy. Because of the flat angle of the glide, even with flaps down, your forward view is poor. If you are not absolutely certain that the runway in front of you is clear, go around.

12. Cut your throttle and land 3-point. If you balloon or bounce, correct by using the throttle. If the balloons or bounces are excessive, apply necessary power and go around. Don't jockey the stick and throttle, because this causes you to crow-hop down the runway.

13. Keep the airplane rolling straight down the runway by using rudder and brakes. Don't try to turn off the runway until the airplane has slowed sufficiently to give you complete control over it. Use the brakes sparingly, but use them if you get into trouble.

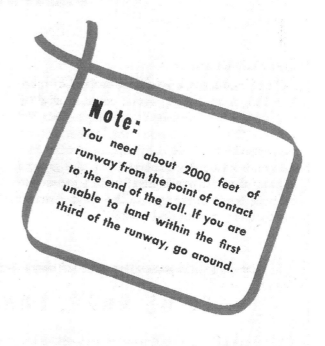

Note: You need about 2000 feet of runway from the point of contact to the end of the roll. If you are unable to land within the first third of the runway, go around.

CROSSWIND, GUSTY, AND WET LANDINGS

Crosswind Landings

When landing in a strong crosswind of more than 15°, or in a gusty wind, come in slightly hot, wheels first, and don't use more than 30° of flaps. The recommended way to correct for crosswind in the P-40 is by dipping a wing into the wind. After the airplane is on the ground be careful not to overcontrol it. In a crosswind the nose tends to swing into the wind. Correct this by using rudder and brakes.

Experienced pilots can make 3-point landings in a crosswind or gusty wind, but it is a maneuver requiring a high degree of skill. To be safe, land wheels first.

Wet Landings

When landing on a wet surface, take it easy with your brakes and controls. Again, a wheels-first landing is your best bet. Use ½ flaps. Taxi slowly and use your brakes sparingly.

TO BE SAFE, LAND WHEELS FIRST

GO-AROUND PROCEDURES

If you want to be an old pilot, **go around** whenever there is the slightest doubt about your approach or landing.

When you start to go around, advance the throttle smoothly to 40″ Hg. and 2600 rpm and climb to 500 feet. Because your flaps are down, it takes longer to gain altitude.

Here is the general procedure:

1. Flap handle in NEUTRAL.
2. Retract landing gear.
3. Fly straight ahead until you reach 500 feet before you make a turn. Don't turn with more than 30° of flaps down unless it is absolutely necessary, and then only with the nose level or down.
4. At 500 feet reduce manifold pressure to 35″ Hg. (33″ Hg. for Grade 91) and 2500 rpm.
5. Don't try to retract the flaps below 500 feet. Here's why: When you put the flap handle in the UP position the flaps rise instantly, thus

causing the airplane to lose altitude before you have enough speed to hold your altitude.

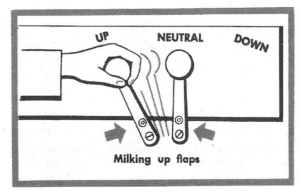

Milking up flaps

6. The best way to retract flaps without losing altitude is by milking them up. To milk up the flaps, rapidly shift the flap handle between the UP and NEUTRAL positions until the flaps are all the way up.

7. Rejoin the traffic pattern and repeat the landing procedure.

LEVEL FLIGHT

For a fighter, the P-40 is an extremely stable airplane in flight—if you trim it right. Remember, periodic adjustments of the trim tabs are necessary as the gas load changes and as speed and power settings vary.

When cruising, keep checking the setting of the trim tabs to see if there is any excessive deviation from NEUTRAL. You may find that you have too much rudder trim and are compensating for it with aileron pressure. This condition is frequent when flying formation.

If your airplane shows a tendency toward excessive wing heaviness, make a note of it in your Form 1A so that the crew chief can adjust the aileron trim tabs. (In P-40's with electric aileron trim tab control you can trim ailerons in flight.)

Your best manifold pressure for cruising is 30″ Hg. (28″ Hg. for Grade 91) and 2300 rpm. At these settings fuel consumption is usually about 50 gallons per hour, varying slightly among individual airplanes.

TURNS

The P-40 has few equals in maneuverability below 15,000 feet. It turns inside nearly all other high-performance fighters. You can make any kind of turn if you coordinate your controls smoothly. Always use a steady pressure on the controls; don't horse back on the stick.

Constant use of the rudder trim tab controls reduces the energy required to work the rudder and makes coordination easier.

Before the P-40 reaches the stalling point in a turn it gives you plenty of warning by shuddering violently. When it begins to shudder,

relax the back pressure on the stick. You can make a turn just above the stalling point, even while the airplane is shuddering, if you coordinate your controls smoothly. Such a turn is a maximum turn. (A higher rpm setting allows you to make a tighter turn.)

A sudden uncoordinated maximum turn usually results in a high-speed stall. If you don't correct the stall immediately, the airplane snaps into a spin. At low altitudes a spin is especially dangerous for you may not have room to pull out of it.

CLIMBS

S CONSTANTLY WHILE CLIMBING

When you climb, right rudder pressure increases. Counteract with rudder trim tab control.

Climb at 35″ Hg. (33″ Hg. for Grade 91) and 2500 rpm. Your best climbing speed is between 150 and 160 mph IAS, but you may climb at a lower indicated airspeed without running any risks.

Your forward visibility is greatly reduced while climbing. S constantly to see what is in front of you.

Don't make tight turns in an ordinary climb, because they reduce your rate of climb considerably. In a climbing turn to the right, you need extra rudder pressure. When you turn to the left, however, you need little rudder pressure. If your IAS decreases, you need more rudder to enter climbing turns.

GLIDES

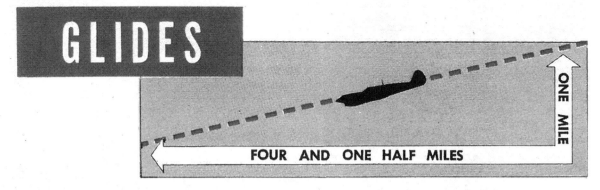

ONE MILE

FOUR AND ONE HALF MILES

The glide ratio for the P-40 with the power off is approximately 4½ feet forward to 1 foot down at a speed of 150 mph with wheels and flaps up and no overload. In other words, from 5280 feet altitude you can glide about 4½ miles.

In an emergency, keep your gliding speed at 150 mph by controlling the angle of your glide. Never let your speed fall below 140 mph. Don't make any turns steeper than 45°.

When practicing long power-on glides, maintain a manifold pressure of at least 20″ Hg. Clear your engine every 2 or 3 minutes to keep the plugs from fouling and the engine from becoming too cold. Don't let your coolant temperature fall below 85°.

When gliding in for a landing use your trim tabs to establish an indicated airspeed of about 110-115 mph.

STALLS

The stalling speed of the P-40 is approximately 84 mph with wheels and flaps down, about 90 mph with wheels and flaps up. (These speeds vary slightly among individual airplanes.)

But you can stall the P-40 at any speed, in any position, if you don't coordinate your controls properly.

If a high-speed stall develops it usually snaps the airplane. Unless you ease back pressure on the stick immediately, the plane goes into a spin. Avoid high-speed stalls. They are dangerous—to you and to the airplane.

Low-speed stalls, on the other hand, are as safe as they were in your AT-6 and are an important part of your P-40 training. Learn low-speed stalls with wheels and flaps up, wheels and flaps down, only wheels down and only flaps down. Low-speed stalls help you to get the feel of your airplane.

If you stall in an unusual position (like the top of a loop or Immelmann) retard the throttle, neutralize the stick and rudder, and wait until the nose is well down before starting recovery.

Do not practice stalls below 8000 feet; you may not have room to recover.

DIVES

YOU NEED 5000 TO 8000 FEET TO RECOVER FROM A HIGH-SPEED DIVE

PULL OUT OF A DIVE FIRMLY AND SMOOTHLY

The P-40 is a great diving airplane. In dives at maximum allowable speeds it has shown no tendency to vibrate, flutter or break to pieces. This doesn't mean that high-speed dives are recommended, particularly at low altitudes. Remember, you need 5000 to 8000 feet to recover from a high-speed dive. The P-40 is red-lined at 480 mph IAS, but while you are in training you should not dive at a speed exceeding 350 mph.

When diving, the P-40 tends to roll to the right. The higher the speed of the dive, the greater the tendency to roll. Compensate by using left rudder pressure and left rudder trim tab control.

All the P-40's except the M and N models have short tails and that means greater rudder and elevator loads. The short-tail models, therefore, require more rudder and elevator pressure.

Pull out of a dive firmly and smoothly. Don't horse back on the stick. A sudden jerky pull-out may throw the airplane into a high-speed stall. This is especially dangerous close to the ground.

Vertical dives from above 20,000 feet are not recommended because of the danger of compressibility.

SPINS

Never spin the P-40 intentionally. Spins in this airplane should be avoided.

Spins in the P-40 are usually a result of one of the following:

1. Tight vertical turns.

2. Uncoordinated turns.

3. Stalling out of the top of the loop or Immelmann.

4. Steep turns at low airspeeds.

It is possible to make the rudder lock in the full left position if you skid the airplane with **almost** full left rudder at a fairly low airspeed, and then suddenly apply power. This may cause a spin. Rudder-load reversals are seldom, if ever, encountered at normal speeds and in normal maneuvers, but if it should happen to you, retard the throttle immediately. With power reduced, you should have no further trouble in centralizing the rudder.

Rudder locking has not been experienced in the P-40's with extended fuselages—the M and N models.

NORMAL SPINS

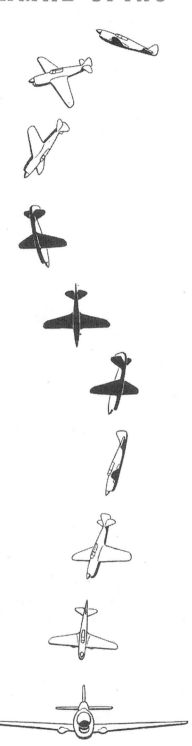

In case of a normal spin, follow this procedure:

1. Retard the throttle.

DIRECTION OF SPIN

2. Apply full opposite rudder to stop the turn.

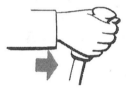

3. Push the stick forward to build up normal diving speed.

4. Don't use the ailerons against the turn, because this has a blanketing action on the rudder surfaces.

5. Pull out of the dive smoothly. Do not hurry the airplane, or it will snap into another spin.

> **NOTE:** If you are unable to break the spin, and if sufficient altitude remains, retard the throttle completely, and take your hands and feet off the controls. The airplane ordinarily recovers by itself in two or three turns.

You lose about 1000 feet per turn in a spin. Recovery takes about 2000 feet after the airplane stops turning.

INVERTED SPINS

To recover from an inverted spin, you must first change the inverted spin into a normal spin, and then recover in the usual manner. Follow this procedure:

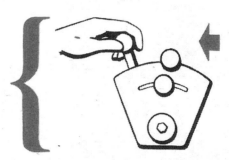

1. Retard the throttle immediately.

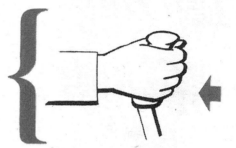

2. Apply full back pressure on the stick.

DIRECTION OF SPIN

3. Apply rudder pressure *with* the spin—not against it.

4. When the airplane goes into a normal spin, follow the normal spin recovery technique.

NOTE: If you can't break an inverted spin, retard the throttle, and take your hands and feet off the controls. The airplane usually recovers by itself after a couple of turns.

NORMAL SPIN RECOVERY PROCEDURES ONLY AGGRAVATE AN INVERTED SPIN

AEROBATICS

You perform aerobatics in a P-40 the same way you did in the AT-6. There are, of course, some differences because of the higher airspeed and increased pressure on the control surfaces of the P-40. But, fundamentally, you will meet no new problems.

The following maneuvers are prohibited

Outside loops.

Slow rolls in excess of 285 mph.

Spins.

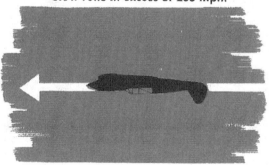

Continuous inverted flight
(because of engine lubrication limitations).

Snap rolls in excess of 140 mph.

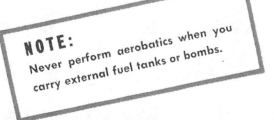

NOTE: Never perform aerobatics when you carry external fuel tanks or bombs.

HERE ARE A FEW TIPS ON AEROBATICS IN THE P-40:

LOOPS

New P-40 pilots sometimes have trouble with loops. They apply too little back pressure on the stick at the beginning of the loop and too much back pressure at the top of the loop. You will find loops easy if you:

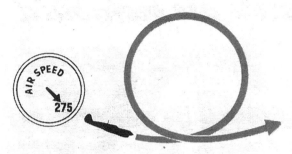

1. Enter the loop at about 275 mph.

2. Greatly increase the back pressure on the stick until the airplane passes beyond the vertical position and you can see the horizon behind you.

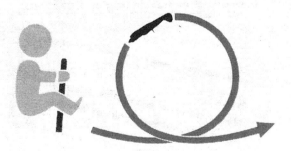

3. Release the back pressure on the stick and allow the airplane to fly itself around the top of the loop.

IMMELMANNS

Start your Immelmann precisely as you start your loop. When rolling out of the top of the Immelmann be sure to give enough right rudder pressure to keep the nose of the airplane from turning left.

BARREL ROLLS AND SLOW ROLLS

Perform barrel rolls and slow rolls between cruising speed and 285 mph—not over 285 mph.

AEROBATICS IN STRING FORMATION

When performing aerobatics in string formation, be sure to observe these rules:

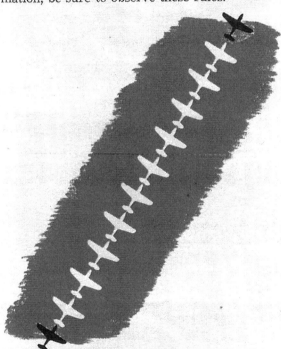

1. Keep about 300 feet (or the length of ten P-40's) between airplanes.
2. Keep the man in front of you in view at all times.
3. Start a maneuver at the exact instant that the man in front of you does. Don't hesitate, waiting to see what he is going to do. If you are alert, you have no doubt about his intentions.

HIGH-ALTITUDE CHARACTERISTICS

The P-40 operates best around 12,000 feet, but you have plenty of occasion to fly at 20,000 feet and higher. Above 15,000 feet there is a marked decrease in reserve engine power. Remember this, especially when you are flying in formation. If you lag behind, it may be impossible to catch up. Be especially careful to hold formation at high altitudes.

To get additional power above 15,000 feet put the mixture control in AUTO LEAN and increase rpm.

Caution: Do not increase rpm past 2600.

On P-40 N's with prop and throttle linkage, your propeller switch must be in FIXED PITCH when you fly above 15,000 feet. Here's why: When you increase the throttle, the propeller setting also increases. Around 15,000 or 16,000 feet the rpm setting jumps to 2700-2900 without a corresponding increase in manifold pressure. By using FIXED PITCH you prevent the rpm from becoming excessive.

When flying formation at high altitudes, remember that the tendency of the airplane to mush and your own tendency to overcontrol increases greatly. Anticipate the need for corrections. Begin correcting sooner at high altitudes than you would at low altitudes. Don't wait too long to correct and then try to make up for lost distance by jockeying the controls.

Perform high-altitude aerobatics with the same airspeeds and with the same control pressures that you use at low altitudes, with one important difference: Because the air is thinner, you need more space to maneuver your airplane.

Vertical dives from above 20,000 feet are not recommended because of the danger of compressibility.

FULL MILITARY LOAD

All P-40 models through the M weigh approximately 9000 lbs. with a full military load. Full military load includes a 75-gallon belly tank and 1470 rounds of .50-cal. ammunition in the wings. The P-40 N, similarly loaded, weighs about 8500 lbs.

Follow these rules when flying with a full military load:

1. Take off with 45″ Hg. and 3000 rpm. Don't try to take off in a 3-point attitude. Get the tail up slightly and fly the airplane off the ground at a speed between 100-105 mph. Retract the landing gear as soon as you are definitely airborne.

2. Climb at a speed of 150-160 mph. When you reach 1000 feet, switch from the fuselage fuel tank to the belly tank and fly on the belly tank until it is empty.

3. Glide about 5 or 10 mph faster than you would with a normal load.

4. Don't exceed 285 mph and never attempt aerobatics when you carry a belly tank.

5. If your engine fails, jettison the belly tank and drop the bombs **safe** before attempting to land. Bomb arming, safe-ing and release handles are located below the throttle quadrant.

6. When landing with a full military load the nose tends to swing to the right. Anticipate this and compensate for it with rudder—and brake, if necessary.

With a 75-gallon belly tank, the total gas supply in the P-40 is 225 gallons. Normal cruising at 30″ Hg. and 2300 rpm allows you a maximum of about 4 hours flight. With 26″ Hg. and 2190 rpm you should have about 4 hours and 30 minutes. For maximum economy, place mixture control in **AUTO LEAN** and don't change the throttle except when absolutely necessary.

The belly tank slows the P-40 down approximately 10 mph.

Emergency Procedures

All the miracles of modern engineering and all the skill of highly trained pilots have not been able to eliminate trouble in the air. Accidents do happen. The P-40 is a well-designed, well-constructed airplane and you are a well-trained pilot, but these facts are no excuse for relaxation. Be alert and be prepared for any emergency.

IN AN EMERGENCY

1. Find out what's wrong with the airplane.

2. Find out whether it can be corrected in the air.

3. If it can be corrected, take immediate measures.

4. If it can't be corrected, land at the nearest field.

If the engine fails completely, but the airplane is controllable and not on fire and if the terrain is reasonably level, it is better to land wheels up than to bail out. The P-40 is strongly built and the cockpit is in a well-protected position. In a belly landing your chances of escaping injury are very good. **Note:** Land into the wind whenever you can.

BAIL OUT ONLY WHEN

1. The plane is out of control or burning.

2. You are flying over water.

3. You are over rough, craggy, or mountainous terrain.

4. You are flying at night—if you can't make an airfield.

FORCED LANDINGS

WITH POWER ON:

If there is an airfield that you can make, land wheels down. If you can't make an airfield, place the landing gear handle in the UP position. Even if the wheels are partly extended they collapse upon impact with the ground.

WITH POWER OFF:

If the engine fails completely and there is any doubt that you can make an airfield, you are better off landing wheels up than wheels down because:

1. You do much less damage to the airplane in a wheels-up landing than if you try a wheels-down landing and mess it up.

2. You personally are in less danger.

3. It is difficult to determine the point of contact on the ground when you land with power off.

Note: It's better to overshoot than undershoot the point of contact.

FORCED LANDING ON TAKEOFF

If the engine fails during takeoff and you have no more than 1000 feet altitude, do not try to turn back to the field. More fighter pilots have been killed trying to turn back to the field after an engine failure during a takeoff than in any other type of forced landing. They invariably try to stretch their glides, thus violating a basic rule of flying.

Instead of turning, **continue straight ahead.** Drop belly tank and bombs, place the landing gear handle UP, lower the flaps and maintain plenty of flying speed.

FORCED LANDING ON AIRFIELDS

When you must make a forced landing on an airfield, stay close enough to the field and keep enough speed and altitude to land wheels down from any angle. If you are approaching the field and have too much altitude, get near the edge of the field and S back and forth until you come down low enough to land.

If you are overshooting, use a nose-low forward slip to lose altitude. The P-40 is an easy airplane to slip and loses altitude fast. When you come in, it's better to overshoot a little than undershoot. You can always lose altitude, but you may find that it's impossible to regain it.

FORCED LANDING AT NIGHT

If you must make a forced landing without power at night and you are near an airfield, try to contact the tower, turn on all landing lights, and come in wheels up.

IF YOU ARE NOT NEAR AN AIRFIELD YOU HAVE ONE CHOICE—*BAIL OUT*.

SWAMPY AND ROUGH TERRAIN

The first rule for landing on rugged terrain is to keep your wheels up. Even if the ground below you seems smooth, land wheels up.

A wheels-up landing requires approximately ⅓ the landing space of a wheels-down landing.

LAND WHEELS DOWN ONLY ON ESTABLISHED AIRFIELDS.

DITCHING

The P-40 is not the best airplane in the world to ditch. If you are at 1000 feet or more and you run into trouble over water, it is generally a better idea to bail out than to ditch.

If you should decide to ditch, follow this procedure:

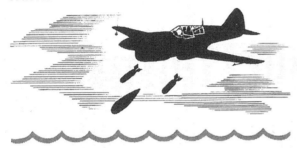

1. Jettison external tanks and drop bombs **safe.**
2. Send out a steady "Mayday" call over your radio.

3. Lean well forward and pull the emergency release on the canopy.
4. Unfasten as many of your parachute straps as you can.
5. Make sure your shoulder harness is locked and your safety belt is securely fastened.
6. You may use flaps to slow your landing, but it is not recommended. They act as diving vanes which tend to force the airplane's nose under water.
7. Establish and maintain a glide at 110 mph.

8. The surface of the water indicates the force and direction of the wind.

a. On a calm surface, land upwind.

b. On a wavy surface with whitecaps but no spray, land along the top of the waves and parallel with the swell.

c. On high waves with foam being whipped into spray, land upwind on the up-slope of the waves.
9. Just before impact, put your left forearm in front of your face to protect yourself against possible flying glass and blows on the face and head.
10. When the airplane is almost stopped, release your safety belt and harness and get out quick. Inflate your Mae West after you have thrown off your parachute harness.

BAILOUTS

There are three generally accepted ways to bail out of a P-40 under control. Each of these methods has its advocates; each has proved successful. It is not the purpose of this manual to tell you which of the three to choose. If the time ever comes, you'll decide in a hurry. Here are the procedures for all three methods of bailing out:

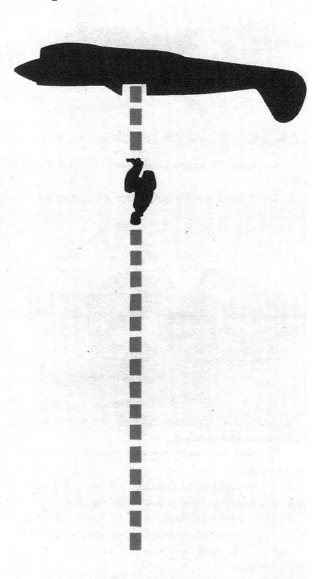

1. The inverted method

a. Roll the canopy back and lock it. If you can't do that, jettison the canopy. Be sure you lean well forward if you jettison the canopy, so that it won't hit you on the head as it flies off.

b. Disconnect your headset and oxygen mask. Put your goggles on.

c. Slow to 170 mph.

d. Trim the airplane nose heavy.

e. Roll the airplane over on its back.

f. Release safety belt and shoulder harness and push out with your hands and feet.

2. Over the side

a. Roll the canopy back or jettison it.

b. Slow the plane to 140 mph.

c. Trim the plane to fly straight and level.

d. Disconnect headset and oxygen mask and put on goggles.

e. Unfasten your safety belt and throw the shoulder harness out of the way.

f. Stand up in the seat using **both hands** to hold onto the airplane. Put your left foot on the front right-hand corner of the open cockpit and dive head-first directly at the trailing edge of the right wing.

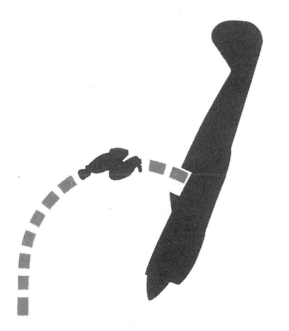

3. Over the nose

a. Roll back the canopy or jettison it.

b. Roll the elevator trim tabs all the way forward. Maintain level flight by using the stick.

c. Disconnect headset and oxygen mask and put on goggles.

d. Loosen safety belt and throw your shoulder harness out of the way.

e. Shove the stick forward. You will be thrown out of the airplane.

If the plane is out of control:

If the plane is in a normal spin, jump over the side. Successful jumps have been made on the inside and outside of spins.

If the plane is in an inverted spin, jettison the canopy and push out with your hands and feet.

FIRE

If fire breaks out during flight, cut all switches and bail out immediately if you have sufficient altitude. If you're too low to bail out, cut the switches and make a wheels-up landing at once, wherever you are. In a forced landing caused by fire, keep the canopy closed as long as possible. When you open the canopy, the flames are whipped into the cockpit.

There is a hand extinguisher in the cockpit, but using the extinguisher during flight is not recommended.

Note: Often a failure of the oil or coolant systems causes the engine to smoke. A smoking engine does not mean the airplane is on fire. You can tell when the airplane is on fire because the cockpit becomes extremely hot.

TIRE FAILURE

If a blowout occurs during takeoff or landing, you can control the airplane with brake and rudder pressure. A good many landings have been made on flat tires without ground-looping the airplane. Remember, the plane tends to turn toward the side on which the tire is flat. Compensate by aileron, rudder, and brake pressure on the opposite side.

EMERGENCY RADIO PROCEDURE

The procedure for transmitting by voice during an emergency is to call "Mayday," give your position as closely as you can figure it, and state your trouble. If you are near an airfield and are going to try to land, call the tower, give your altitude, approximate distance and direction from the field, and the nature of your trouble.

A tone signal carries farther than a voice signal. If possible, tap out an SOS.

Tactical Training

FORMATION FLYING

The importance of formation flying cannot be stressed too strongly. If there is one lesson to be learned from this war it is the absolute necessity of perfect teamwork in flying. The success of the P-40 in Burma during the days of the American Volunteer Group is a prime example of what can be done with faultless formation flying. Outnumbered, fighting against enemy planes with much greater maneuverability, the AVG P-40's were nevertheless able to pile up an incredible score against the Japs. The answer was teamwork, formation.

You get training in precision formation flying with the P-40. Precision formation is to the AAF what drills and reviews are to the infantry. Until planes can fly and fight together as units, they are worthless in modern air war. The purpose of formation flying is to mass airplanes for maximum efficiency, both in attack and defense.

When you learn precision formation flying you are learning the fundamentals of tactical formation flying; you must know precision formations to learn tactical formations. The formation flying you learn now has a direct bearing on the flying you will do in combat. Constant practice in precision flying now really pays off later.

CLOSE FORMATION

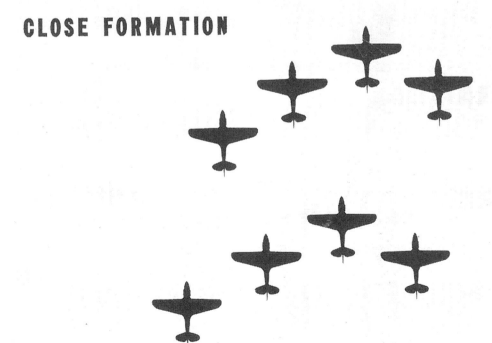

TACTICAL FORMATION

COLUMN FORMATION

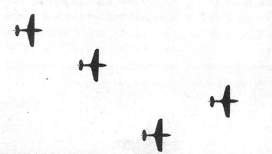

PRECISION FORMATION TECHNIQUE

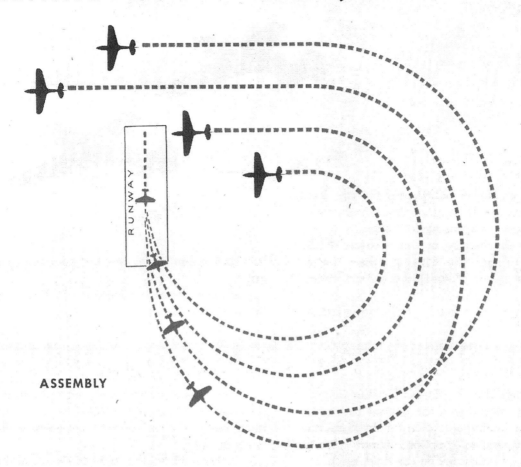

ASSEMBLY

1. Before the flight, be sure you know exactly what is expected of you in your particular position.

2. Start the engine on a pre-arranged signal.

3. Don't taxi dangerously close to other aircraft.

4. Immediately after takeoff, turn the radio volume up. Maintain constant radio contact with the flight.

5. After the takeoff, join formation in a left or right climbing turn. Cut across the circle to expedite assembly. Don't lag behind or try to overhaul by use of power only. Locate every ship in the formation ahead of you. Come in from slightly below, smoothly instead of with a burst of speed.

6. Always slide to the outside of the turn after assembling if there are others to assemble behind you.

Rules for flying formation:

a. The cleanness and high speed of the P-40 cause you to over-run, particularly in closing up on the flight commander's airplane. When you over-run, ease well out to the side on a level with the rest of the formation and slow the airplane down. Do not get directly below, above, or in front of the formation when you over-run because you will lose sight of the flight.

b. Make all changes of position smoothly and slowly. Remember, there are other airplanes behind you.

c. The P-40 moves sideways much more readily than trainer airplanes. You must be alert against the danger of skidding into a lead ship.

d. Overcontrolling, improper use of the throttle, and failure to anticipate maneuvers are the basic causes of poor formation flying

and accidents. Never jockey your throttle, keep your eyes on the flight at all times, and relieve control pressures by using trim tabs.

e. Make all changes in the position of the formation so that the wingman does not go blind on the leader. **Make all cross-overs underneath.**

f. If you get into trouble while flying forma-tion, leave the formation by going down and out.

g. Always know the position of other aircraft in the formation.

Landing:

a. The flight leader obtains landing instructions for the flight from the control tower. He controls the landing operation for the flight and relays pertinent information (wind velocity, crosswinds, obstructions on the field, etc.).

b. After peeling off for the landing, establish the proper interval on the downwind leg.

c. The flight leader lands on one side of the runway, the second man on the opposite side; the whole flight continues to alternate in this manner. The purpose of this procedure is to get the planes down quickly, to stay out of prop wash and to clear the plane in front of you in case of an accident.

d. Don't land dangerously close behind the man in front of you. (As proficiency of the flight improves, the time interval between landings is reduced.)

e. After landing, the flight leader should taxi clear of the runway to a safe position (at least 150 feet to the side and heading away from the runway). Thus he can go straight ahead in case any plane in the flight gets out of control while landing.

f. Radio contact should be maintained after the landing until every one of the airplanes is parked on the line and all the engines have been shut off.

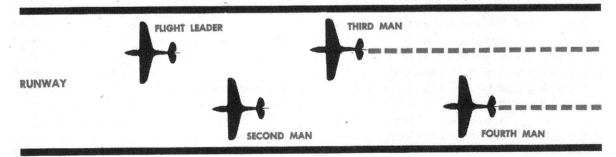

SIGNALS

The following formation signals are standard throughout the AAF:

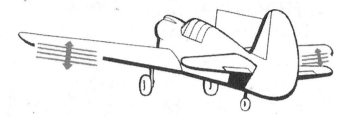

1. Ready for takeoff
Moving the ailerons up and down.

2. Assembly
Rocking of wings.

3. Open up or loosen formation
Fishtail (use the rudder only).

4. Echelon left
Dipping the left wing.

5. Echelon right
Dipping the right wing.

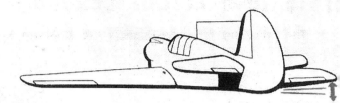

6. Attention!
Expect a rapid maneuver
Rapid fluttering of the ailerons.

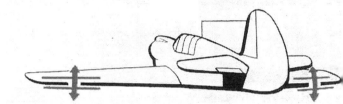

7. Landing
Pumping of the elevators.

8. Switch to a full tank of gas
Rotating the wrist as though turning a selector valve.

NOTE: Signals for string formation vary at different installations.

HINTS TO A FLIGHT LEADER
If you are chosen to lead a flight, here are some things to remember:

1. Always start a maneuver smoothly and never more quickly than the proficiency of your flight warrants.

2. Emphasize proficiency and smoothness in all your flying. Violent or erratic movements, excessive use of the throttle, and lack of consideration for the man behind you cause the men in the formation to lose their respect for your leadership.

3. Always leave a reserve of power and speed for your wingmen. For example, with the flight in echelon, reduce throttle before turning steeply away from the flight.

4. Use the radio sparingly. Employ visual signals as much as possible.

5. Don't baby your formation. As the proficiency of your wingmen develops, make your maneuvers more difficult. Remember, anything that can be done in a single airplane can be done, with proper handling, in a formation. Aimless cruising around and timid maneuvering are wastes of time.

6. Don't exceed the capabilities of your wingmen. Don't try to show the flight that you are a hot pilot.

7. Don't look for trouble. You are responsible for every man in the formation, as well as for yourself. Let that responsibility guide all your actions.

8. When leading a formation composed of more than two flights, make a 45° turn away from the direction of your assembly turn immediately after the takeoff; then make your assembly turn.

9. Always hold a critique immediately after the formation lands.

PROPELLER SHADOW

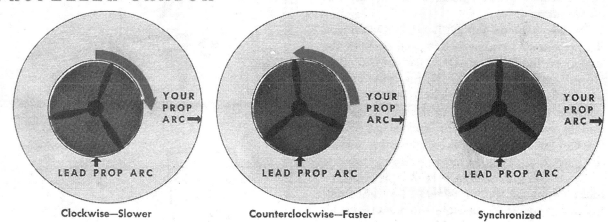

Clockwise—Slower   Counterclockwise—Faster   Synchronized

If your tachometer should fail while you are flying formation, and you want to know what rpm you are using, sight through the arc of your propeller at the propeller of the lead airplane. Note the shadow of the propeller. If the shadow rotates clockwise, your propeller is turning **slower** than the lead airplane's propeller. If the shadow rotates counter-clockwise, your propeller is turning **faster.**

If the shadow is stopped, you are perfectly synchronized with the lead airplane.

When the shadow is rotating in either direction, vary the pitch of your propeller until the shadow stops.

GUNNERY

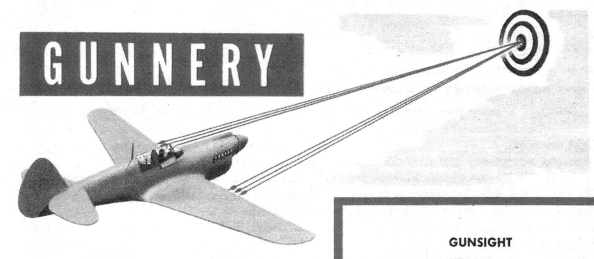

The P-40 is armed with six free-firing .50-cal. machine guns, three in each wing. Each gun must be charged manually on the ground. Each gun carries 235 rounds—approximately 10 seconds' continuous firing.

The electrical ring-and-dot optical gunsight is mounted directly in front of your face. To operate the gunsight, place the gunsight breaker switch in the ON position and turn on the gunsight rheostat switch. A transparent green sunshield can be raised over the gunsight's reflector glass by a lever on the left side of the sight.

To fire, turn on the ALL GUN switch and the armament breaker switch, and squeeze the trigger on the forward part of the control stick. On all models except the N, the guns can be fired two at a time. From right to left, the inside breaker switch controls the inboard guns; the middle switch controls the middle guns; and the end switch controls the outboard guns. On the P-40 N all six guns must be fired at once.

The P-40's gun camera is an N-2 or N-6 type mounted on the leading edge of the right landing gear fairing. To operate the camera on all models except N, turn the No. 4 breaker switch to ON and turn on the gun camera switch above the ignition switch. In the P-40 N, turn the No. 3 breaker switch to ON and turn on the ALL-GUN switch. In the N, the camera is combined with the ALL-GUN switch. Normal loading for the gun camera is about 50 feet of film—approximately 15 seconds' shooting time.

GUNSIGHT

You can move your head in relation to this sight without disturbing the alignment of sight and target. Both move together, which gives you considerably more freedom of movement and eliminates the need to keep everything perfectly aligned.

Head in center

Head to left   Head to right

HINTS ON GUNNERY

It is not within the scope of this manual to deal with the science of aerial gunnery. Many excellent books, pamphlets and tech orders have been written about gunnery—sources that you would be wise to consult. Unless you understand gunnery, unless you can hit your target, you are worthless as a fighter pilot. A fighter airplane is a flying gun platform. It has one purpose: to destroy the enemy. Similarly, all the training you have gone through up to now has had one purpose: to teach you to position your airplane for firing.

The P-40, like all fighter airplanes, was designed for gunnery. If you observe the following rules while firing in the P-40, you will find your gunnery techniques easy to master:

1. Fly smoothly while sighting at the target.

2. At the proper firing speed, trim the airplane to fly practically hands off.

3. Don't get too close to the target: you may mush into it on the pullout.

4. Never fire a burst at a tow target longer than 3 seconds; a longer burst is harmful to your guns.

APPROACHES

Three basic approaches are employed for firing at any target in the air. There are, of course, variations of each approach, but until you master the basic three you cannot become proficient at the variations. The three approaches are:

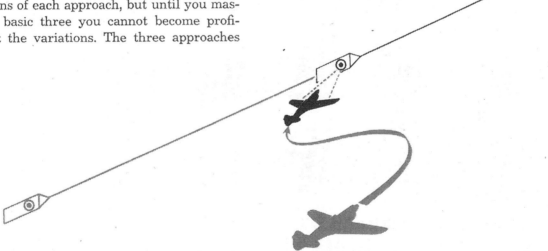

1. 90° SIDE APPROACH

Position your airplane so that the target is 45° behind you, about 800 yards out to the side. Make a steady progressive turn into the target until you reach a point 90° from the target's line of flight and in the correct range. At this point bring your sight up to the target from behind, ready for sighting. Concentrate on the

sight so that while you continue your turn, you draw the bead of the sight through the target until you have the correct deflection. When the range, line of flight, and deflection are all correct, fire.

Note: Your must fly your airplane **smoothly** during the pay-off stage of the attack.

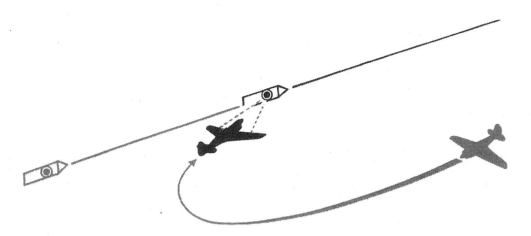

2. 180° SIDE APPROACH

The difference between the 180° side approach and the 90° side approach is the greatly increased rate of closure. Start your turn into the target when the towing airplane is about 15° in front of you. You should have completed 90° of your turn and be almost within range of the target when it comes abreast of you. Continue your turn, fly very smoothly, and pull the bead of your sight through the target until you have the proper deflection. When your range, your line of flight, and deflection are all correct, fire.

Break away from the target by chandelling up and over. In the 180° side approach, never get below the target and never fire at an angle of less than 20°.

3. OVERHEAD APPROACH OR PASS

Position yourself about 2500 feet above the target and far enough ahead so that you can see it just behind the trailing edge of the wing. Pull your airplane into a climbing turn into the target until your IAS is about 150 mph. Increase the rate of your turn and drop your nose below the horizon until you are directly behind the target and diving at it at an angle of about 45°. (Keep the target in sight at all times.) Draw the bead of sight through the target until you have the proper deflection and correct range. Fire.

Important: After firing, recover to the side of the target from which you started the attack. Do not recover behind, below, or forward of the target and towing airplane.

Caution: When you are attacking at 270 mph your left rudder pressure increases. Anticipate this increase and compensate for it by using rudder trim tabs.

BOMBING

This airplane is equipped to carry one bomb under each wing, plus one bomb in the belly tank position. To arm the bombs, put the bomb arming handle on the floor below the throttle quadrant in the ARM position. To release the bombs, there are manual release handles on the left side of the cockpit.

Auxiliary gas tanks may be carried in place of the bombs under each wing and fuselage. These tanks range in capacity from 52 to 150 gallons.

The needs of war have forced the P-40 into all sorts of bombing techniques. Often the P-40 has doubled as a light bomber or an attack plane. It has carried bombs up to 1000 lbs. But ordinarily, the P-40 is used for two types of bombing—dive bombing and minimum-altitude bombing.

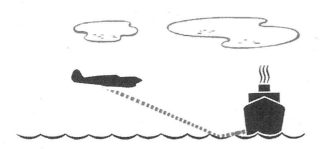

MINIMUM-ALTITUDE BOMBING

Minimum-altitude or skip bombing is the most accurate kind that can be done with a fighter. Although this type of bombing has been performed from levels of only a few feet, you should not go below 50 feet for training purposes. Many unorthodox techniques and many rules you won't find in any book have been successful in minimum-altitude bombing in combat, so it is not the kind of thing that you can describe with a series of set principles. There are, however, these basic rules:

1. You should maintain a straight and level approach for at least 5 seconds before the bomb is released.

2. Try to undershoot the target, because undershooting allows the bomb to skip into its target.

3. Always use delayed action bombs. They give the airplane time to get out of danger before the explosion, and they delay the explosion until the bomb can skip into the target.

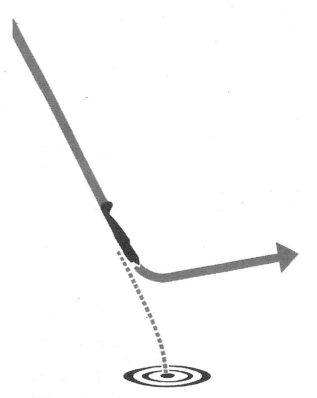

DIVE BOMBING

In dive bombing you arm your bombs just before beginning the approach. Come over the target at 4500 feet, pull up and slow the airplane to 150 mph. Roll over and start your dive. Be sure the airplane is properly trimmed for high speed so that it won't be necessary to use much left rudder. Don't dive faster than 350 mph IAS.

Put the bead of your gunsight on the center of the target as you dive. The angle of the dive should not be greater than 70° or smaller than 45°. Just as you start the pullout, release the bomb.

While in training, pull out at 2000 feet above the earth—never less than 1000 feet. Don't horse back on the stick during the pullout because you might get into a high-speed stall.

NAVIGATION

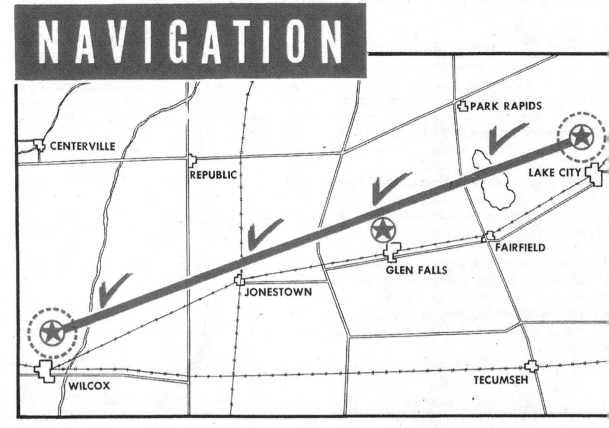

Here are some pointers to help you navigate in the P-40

1. The P-40 travels 50 to 60 mph faster than the AT-6, so you have to check your time intervals more closely and carefully. Bear in mind that your IAS increases 2% every 1000 feet. If your airspeed indicator shows 200 mph at 15,000 feet, you are actually traveling at a ground-speed of 260 mph (with no wind).

2. When you are planning to make a cross country flight, draw a penciled line along your proposed route and follow it as closely as possible. Mark check points on the penciled line at approximately 15-minute intervals. For check points, choose large, easily identified landmarks, because your speed makes it necessary to recognize landmarks in a hurry. Rivers, railroad tracks and towns make good check points.

3. Do not fly in bad weather over unfamiliar terrain unless it is absolutely necessary.

4. Know the capacity of each fuel tank and how long it takes to consume the fuel in each

tank at the 50-60 gallon per hour normal rate with a constant power setting. Remember that in formation flying, when your power setting constantly changes, your fuel consumption is considerably greater than during normal level flight.

Plan no flight longer than 2 hours unless you carry a belly tank. If you are flying with a belly tank, use it first. The 75-gallon belly tank normally lasts about 1 hour and 10 minutes. Check the proper functioning of all fuel tanks on the ground; immediately after the takeoff fly a minute on each tank to make sure it is working right.

5. Learn to use radio navigation aids; they may save your life someday. The Technical Order 30-100 series, which you have, deals in great detail with radio navigational aids. It pays to spend some time studying these Technical Orders. The more you know about navigation the better your chances of getting there and back.

LOST PROCEDURES

IF YOU GET LOST:

1. For maximum economy reduce the manifold pressure to 26″ Hg. and the rpm setting to 2190.

2. Come down to an altitude between 1000 and 500 feet and look around for towns and landmarks which you might identify on your map. You can usually find the name of a town painted on a water tower, standpipe or railroad station.

3. Use your radio. If you have VHF, try to contact a station on the B channel and request an emergency homing. If you can't get any response on your VHF, turn on your Detrola. You can't transmit on the Detrola, but you can receive control towers and radio beams. Tune in on the strongest beam signal you can find, and follow it in for a landing. If you have an SCR 274 set, tune it to a beam and follow it in.

4. If you see an airfield, try to contact the tower with your radio. (If you have VHF, use the B channel.) **If you fail to establish radio contact, come in and land.**

INSTRUMENT FLYING

Technical Order Series 30-100 is the bible of instrument flying. You have it. Use it.

Proficiency in instrument flying is life insurance. Wherever you are, whatever type airplane you are flying, you may have to use instruments. Never get out of practice.

Here are a few tips that should help you if you get caught in bad weather and have to fly instruments:

1. Your instruments work better at slower speeds. Slow your airplane and lower ¼ flaps.

2. Increase your rpm setting to 2600.

3. If you want to climb, climb at a speed of about 160 mph.

4. Make up your mind about how you are going to try to get out of the weather. Will you turn around, climb above or let down? When you have made a decision, stick to it. Don't change suddenly from a climb to a let-down, or vice versa. A panicky maneuver gets you into plenty of trouble.

5. Here are your best indicated airspeeds:

Cruise	175 mph
Climb	150-160 mph
Let-down	140-150 mph

NIGHT FLYING

The technique of night flying is closely related to instrument flying. A few suggestions:

1. Know the location of your controls, instruments and switches.

2. Always carry a flashlight.

3. Be super-careful when taxiing. Use your landing light intermittently except in extremely congested areas. Never use your landing light for more than 10 seconds at one time.

4. Use side spotlights for reading maps and charts.

5. Check all cockpit lights before leaving the line.

6. Make an accurate check on your flight instruments.

7. Keep the cockpit lights dim to avoid losing the horizon.

8. On an especially dark night you may have trouble finding the horizon. Turn on all gyro flight instruments and check them frequently.

9. Do absolutely no acrobatics.

10. Know the location of emergency landing fields in the area over which you are flying.

NIGHT TAKEOFF

The things you have to remember when taking off at night are these:

1. Be sure your running lights are on before starting the engine.

2. If you use your landing light for taxiing, remember to retract it before starting the takeoff, or immediately after takeoff.

3. Keep all your cockpit lights turned low.

4. When taking off, pick a point on the horizon in front of you and hold to that point so that you can take off on a straight course.

NIGHT LANDING

1. All your cockpit lights should be dim.

2. You are safer landing wheels first than 3-point because of reduced visibility and your own tendency to level off high at night.

3. Whether you land with your landing light on or off is up to you. Some pilots always use their landing lights; others say that having the light on causes a glare on the runway. If you plan to use the landing light, extend it after your last turn into the field. Do not extend the landing light when you are flying over 140 mph.

Caution:

The landing light should not be used when there is fog on the ground because:

1. Glare and blindness may result.

2. Depth perception is distorted.

3. You may mistake the top of the fog for the ground.

TECHNICAL ORDERS FOR THE P-40

AIRCRAFT AND MAINTENANCE PARTS

P-40E-1

01-25CF-1 . . . . Pilots Flight Operating Instructions
01-25CJ-2 . . . . Erection and Maintenance Instructions
01-25CJ-3 . . . . Overhaul Instructions
01-25CJ-4 . . . . Parts Catalogue

P-40F and P-40L

01-25CH-1 . . . . Pilots Flight Operating Instructions
01-25CH-2 . . . . Erection and Maintenance Instructions
01-25CH-4 . . . . Parts Catalogue (F model)
01-25CL-4 . . . . Parts Catalogue (L model)

P-40K and P-40M

01-25CK-1 . . . . Pilots Flight Operating Instructions
01-25CK-2 . . . . Erection and Maintenance Instructions
01-25CK-3 . . . . Overhaul Instructions
01-25CK-4 . . . . Parts Catalogue

P-40N

01-25CN-1 . . . . Pilots Flight Operating Instructions
01-25CN-2 . . . . Erection and Maintenance Instructions
01-25C-4 . . . . Parts Catalogue

ENGINES AND MAINTENANCE PARTS

P-40E-1, P-40K, P-40M, and P-40N

02-5AB-2 . . . . Service Instructions
02-5AB-3 . . . . Overhaul Instructions
02-5AB-4 . . . . Parts Catalogue

P-40F and P-40L

02-55AA-2 . . . . Service Instructions
02-55AA-3 . . . . Overhaul Instructions
02-55AA-4 . . . . Parts Catalogue

Index

	Page
Aerobatics	65-66
loops	66
Immelmanns	66
in string formation	66
After takeoff	53
Ammeter	16
Bailouts	74-75
Bombing	87
minimum altitude	87
dive bombing	87
Brakes	30
parking brake handle	30
Breaker switches	17
Canopy	37
Checklists	39-43
cockpit	40
engine warmup	43
external	39
starting	41-42
stopping	42
Climbs	59
Cockpit	37-38
Cold weather tips	44
Control surfaces	8
Coolant system	22
shutters	22
temperature gage	22
Description, general	7
Detonation	9
Dimensions	7
Ditching	73
Dives	61
Electrical system	16-17
Emergency procedures	69-76
Engine	9-12
Allison	9
Rolls Royce	11
Engine primer	12

	Pag
Fire	
Flaps	
control	
indicators	
Flight characteristics	49-6
Flying Tigers	
Forced landings	71-
at night	
on airfields	
on swampy and rough terrain	
on takeoff	
with power off	
with power on	
Formation flying	77-8
hints to flight leader	8
precision technique	7
signals	81, 8
Fuel system	18-1
gages	
selector valve	
tank capacities	
vented tank	
Full military load	6
Generator reset button	1
Glides	6
Go around procedures	5
Grade 91 Fuel	47-4
Gun Camera	8
Gunsight	8
Gunnery	84-8
approaches	85-8
Heating	3
High altitude characteristics	6
Hot weather tips	4
Hydraulic system	23-3
auxiliary pump	2
emergency pump	2
Ignition switch	1

Page

Instrument flying 89
Landing gear 24-28
    lowering 26-27
    retracting 24-25
    wheel indicators 29
Landings 54-56
    crosswind, gusty, and wet landings......56
Level flight 58
Lighting 38
Lost procedures 89
Manifold pressure gage..................12
Manifold pressure regulator..................9
Mixture control 11
Navigation 88-89
Night flying 90
    landing 90
    takeoff 90
Oil system 20-21
    overheating 21
    pressure gage 20
    tank 21
    temperature gage 20
Oxygen equipment 35-36
    constant flow 36
    demand system 35-36
Power settings 45-48
    Allison engine 45, 48
    Rolls Royce engine..................46, 48

Page

Pre-takeoff check 51
Propeller 13-15
    breaker switch 13
    control 13
    selector switch 14
    trouble 15
Propeller shadow 83
Radio 31-34
    emergency procedure..................34, 76
    microphone 34
    SCR 274-N 33-34
    VHF 31-32
Seating 38
Spins 62-64
    inverted 64
    normal 63
Stalls 60
Starter 12
Supercharger 11
Tachometer 12
Takeoff 52
Taxiing 50
Throttle quadrant 11
Tire failure 76
Tomahawk 6
Trim tabs 8
Turns 58
Warhawk 6

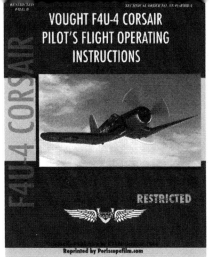
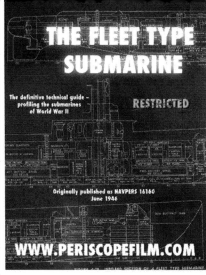
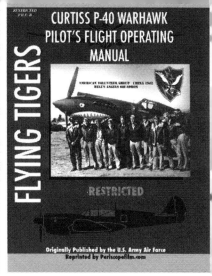
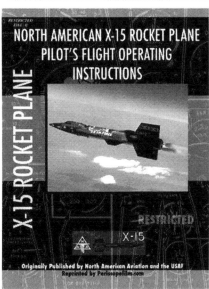
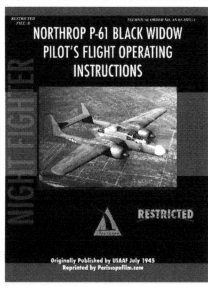
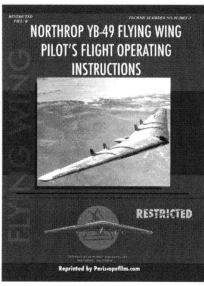

HUGHES FLYING BOAT
MANUAL

SPRUCE GOOSE

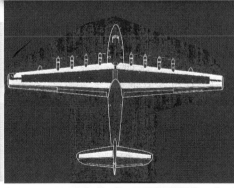

RESTRICTED

Originally Published by the War Department
Reprinted by Periscope Film LLC

NOW AVAILABLE!

Printed in Great Britain
by Amazon